WELCO

FOOTBALL LEGENDS:
THE FORWARDS EDITION

Lunar Press is an independent publishing company that cares greatly about the accuracy of its content.

If you notice any inaccuracies or have anything that you would like to discuss, then please email us at lunarpresspublishers@gmail.com.

Enjoy!

© Copyright 2024 - All rights reserved.
The content contained within this book may not be reproduced, duplicated or transmitted without direct written permission from the author or the publisher.

Under no circumstances will any blame or legal responsibility be held against the publisher, or author, for any damages, reparation, or monetary loss due to the information contained within this book, either directly or indirectly.

Legal Notice:
This book is copyright protected. It is only for personal use. You cannot amend, distribute, sell, use, quote or paraphrase any part, or the content within this book, without the consent of the author or publisher.

Disclaimer Notice:
Please note the information contained within this document is for educational and entertainment purposes only. All effort has been executed to present accurate, up to date, reliable, complete information. No warranties of any kind are declared or implied. Readers acknowledge that the author is not engaged in the rendering of legal, financial, medical or professional advice. The content within this book has been derived from various sources. Please consult a licensed professional before attempting any techniques outlined in this book.

By reading this document, the reader agrees that under no circumstances is the author responsible for any losses, direct or indirect, that are incurred as a result of the use of the information contained within this document, including, but not limited to, errors, omissions, or inaccuracies.

IF YOU ENJOY THIS BOOK, CHECK OUT...

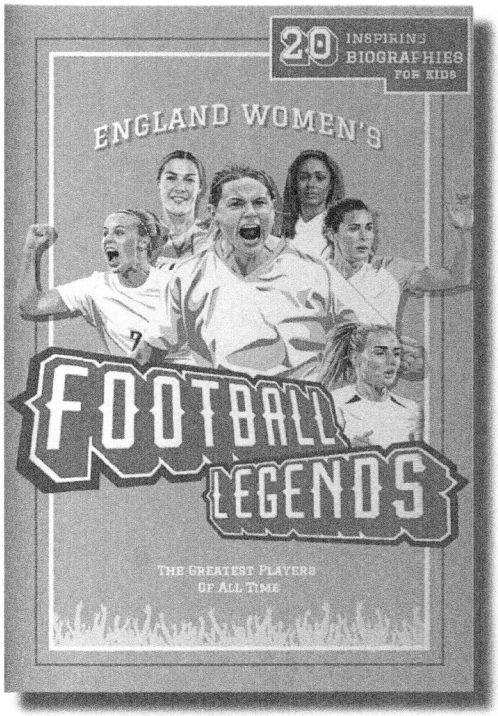

Dive deeper into the Football Legends universe with *England Women's Football Legends: 20 Inspiring Biographies for Kids*.

The England women's football team **made history, broke down barriers and shattered records**, but their journey to greatness hasn't been easy.

Their stories are ones of perseverance and courage, and **we hope these legends inspire you.**

CONTENTS

Pelé	6
Cristiano Ronaldo	12
Robert Lewandowski	19
Ronaldo	25
Gerd Müller	31
Ferenc Puskás	36
Lionel Messi	41
Ronaldinho	47
Eusébio	53
Alfredo Di Stéfano	59
Luís Figo	65
Marco van Basten	71
Thierry Henry	77
Romário	82
Rivaldo	87
Luis Suárez	93
Raúl	99
Roberto Baggio	105
George Best	111
Diego Maradona	117

KICK OFF

Deciding who is the greatest forward in history is nearly impossible, as there have been so many legendary players. That's why this list isn't numbered. It's a collection of 20 world-class forwards, with each and every one of them in with a shout of being the best! Deciding who goes where on the list can be your job...

Of course, many amazing players didn't make our list, and others didn't make the cut as it was hard to decide if they were midfielders or attackers. Should Zinedine Zidane be classed as a forward or a creative midfielder? The same can be said for Johan Cruyff and Paul Scholes.

But we're here to celebrate the 20 who did make the list, and you will have trouble finding fault with any of them!

Football has been around for a long, long time, so there have been thousands of attacking superstars through the years. Cutting the list of the best is harder than picking players for it, as it can be heartbreaking to leave off legends such as Neymar, Alan Shearer and Karim Benzema.

Also, there are the likes of Kylian Mbappé, who will surely make such a list in years to come, but he is probably a little early in his career to be considered a true great just yet.

You might not have seen footage of some of the players on this list, or maybe you're football crazy and spend your downtime watching highlight reels of Puskas, Müller and Marco van Basten. Either way, the info on how good these older players were is on these pages, so their stories are here for you to enjoy.

To get to the top of any sport is ridiculously hard, but to do it in football, the most popular sport in the world, is next to impossible. That's why the things these players have achieved are amazing. They are the best of the best!

Still, it's not all about trophies, as some players such as George Best played for Northern Ireland, who were never going to win—or even qualify for—a World Cup. He still won things with his club, but the ultimate prize was not an option. He is remembered for his unreal talent and skills on the pitch.

Anyway, it's time for you to dig in and learn about 20 of the greatest forwards in the history of football! Can you decide who is the best of the best? Enjoy!

EDSON
ARANTES DO NASCIMENTO

PELÉ

Teams

SANTOS
1956–1974
APPS – 1207, GLS – 1165

NEW YORK COSMOS
1975–1977
APPS – 64, GLS – 37

Trophy Cabinet

WORLD CUP	X3
BRAZILIAN CHAMPION	X6
COPA LIBERTADORES	X2
INTERCONTINENTAL CUP	X2
NASL SOCCER BOWL	X1

International Stats

CAPS	GOALS
92	77

BIOGRAPHY

BORN	OCT 23, 1940
NATIONALITY	BRAZILIAN
STRONG FOOT	RIGHT
HEIGHT	1.73M
RETIRED	OCT 1, 1977

As mentioned in the introduction, this list will not be numbered because it is just too hard to separate these great players. That final decision is yours! Still, it seems fitting to start with Pelé, the man many people claim was the best. At the very least, he was the first global superstar in football, and he made the yellow Brazilian kit the most dreamed-about Christmas present for kids around the world for decades!

Apart from being the original superstar, Pelé was also an unbelievable player. Along with his shockingly high goal-scoring records, he was a three-time World Cup winner. That's right—he won the World Cup three times!

Before all of that, Edson Arantes do Nascimento (or as we know him, simply Pelé) was born on 23 October 1940 in Três Corações, a small town wedged between Brazil's two biggest cities, São Paulo and Rio de Janeiro. His father was a semi-professional footballer, so Pelé was raised surrounded by the game he would grow up to dominate.

His parents gave him his original first name, Edson, in honour of the great American inventor Thomas Edison. There was a mix-up at the hospital the day Pelé was born, and whoever filled out the birth certificate forgot to add the "i", so Edison became Edson!

Another funny story surrounds his nickname, Pelé. When he was a kid, his favourite player was Bilé, who played in goal for Vasco da Gama. He was too young to pronounce Bilé's name correctly, and it came out as "Pelé", which then became the name his friends called him! It stuck, and the Brazilian legend Pelé was born!

Pelé grew up in poverty, and even as a child, he had to work part-time after school as a servant for local rich families. His father was only semi-pro, so he didn't earn much money at all. When Pelé wasn't in school or working, he was playing football—constantly.

Sadly, his family and all of his neighbours couldn't afford a proper football, so Pelé used to practise with a sock stuffed with old newspapers or, if that wasn't available, a grapefruit.

When he was ten, Pelé had his first taste of World Cup fever. Brazil were the host nation for the 1950 World Cup, and they were the firm favourites. When they reached the final to play Uruguay, their fierce neighbours, everyone expected Brazil to win. The national newspapers even printed things like BRAZIL ARE CHAMPIONS! and WORLD CUP GLORY!

Back before the internet, news stories were printed the night before and sent to the shops the following morning. After Brazil were shocked by Uruguay, losing 2—1, everyone woke up to the false news that Brazil were world champions!

The night of the final, Pelé's father and loads of his neighbours gathered around the one transistor radio the village had. When Brazil lost, everyone was devastated. Pelé saw his father crying for the first and only time in his life. He told his dad not to worry, and that one day, Pelé would win him a World Cup. He won him three!

As a teen, Pelé was a **prodigy**, ripping up the local scene and scoring buckets of goals. He took part in the first-ever **futsal** tournament, the version of football that is so Brazilian it should wear a yellow strip! Futsal is played with a smaller ball, which means the players need better close control and touch. It's led to the Brazilian players always having silky skills.

One of his youth coaches, an ex-Brazilian international named Waldemar de Brito, believed Pelé was like nothing he'd seen before. He recommended him to Santos, one of the biggest clubs in Brazil, and Pelé was signed up at 15. He made his debut soon after and scored a goal in a 7–1 demolition of Corinthians.

In his first full season (he was only 16!), Pelé played most games, and he finished the year as the league's top scorer. Ten months after making his Santos debut, he was called up to the Brazil team, which shot him into world news. At a time when players rarely left their own country to join other teams, sides like Real Madrid and Manchester United started scouting Pelé.

In fact, Inter Milan came very close to getting him, and Santos even accepted a bid. When the Santos fans found out, they rioted, and the contract was torn up!

Spanish side Valencia then had a bid accepted, and it was agreed that Pelé would join them after the 1958 World Cup. That all changed when Pelé, just 17, shredded every defence he faced in Sweden, where the World Cup was being held. He scored throughout the tournament but saved the best for last, netting twice in the final. He was just 17, making him the youngest player in history to play in a World Cup final.

His first goal of the game, where he flicked a bouncing ball over a Swedish defender's head before volleying it into the net, is still considered one of the greatest goals of all time. One of the Swedish players admitted years later that he had to stop himself from applauding.

Following the World Cup and the crazy fame that fell on Pelé, Santos told Valencia that the deal was off. There would be riots all over Brazil if they sold him.

The 1962 World Cup in Chile was the biggest yet, mainly because everyone wanted to see Pelé, who was now 21. Sadly, it ended up being the worst World Cup in history, with most of the games becoming nothing more than cage fights, with broken legs, bloodied noses and cut faces a regular thing. Pelé got the worst of it, and he was kicked out of the tournament in the second game. Brazil won the World Cup, but Pelé missed most of it.

By the 1970 World Cup, Brazil were said to be past it. Pelé was getting on in years, and most of his teammates from the successful '58 and '62 wins had retired. In fact, Pelé had thought about retiring, too, but had been talked out of it. In his new number 10 role, he dropped deeper, threading passes through for his teammates and chipping in with the odd goal.

Brazil were incredible, and the first World Cup to be

shown around the world in colour blasted Pelé and the Brazilian team to a fame never before seen. Every kid wanted a yellow football strip, and they all wanted to be Pelé when they played on their local pitches! If you've never watched World Cup 1970 highlights, then get on YouTube as soon as you're done with this book. You won't regret it.

In his time with Santos, where he spent nearly all of his club career, Pelé won the league six times, including five times in a row in the early 1960s. He won the Copa Libertadores (South American Champions League) twice and the Intercontinental Supercup once. He won three World Cups with Brazil, scoring 77 goals in just 92 international games. His goal-scoring record stood until it was beaten by Neymar, who needed 125 games to score the same number of goals.

Pelé finished his career in America, becoming one of the first stars to play in Major League Soccer (MLS). He won the league in 1977 before retiring to take up a role as a global ambassador* for football. He scored 1,279 goals in 1,363 career games, which is a world record.

In December 2000, Pelé was voted as the greatest player of all time alongside Diego Maradona. They couldn't be split. Pelé died at 82 after a long battle with cancer. He is truly one of the greatest players ever to kick a ball.

CRISTIANO RONALDO
DOS SANTOS AVEIRO

Teams

SPORTING CP
2002–2003
APPS – 25, GLS – 3
↓
MANCHESTER UNITED
2003–2009
APPS – 196, GLS – 84
↓
REAL MADRID
2009–2018
APPS – 292, GLS – 311
↓
JUVENTUS
2018–2021
APPS – 98, GLS – 81
↓
MANCHESTER UNITED
2021–2022
APPS – 40, GLS – 19
↓
AL NASSR
2023–
APPS – 47, GLS – 49

Trophy Cabinet

EUROS	X1
BALLON D'OR	X5
CHAMPIONS LEAGUE	X5
PREMIER LEAGUE	X3
LA LIGA CHAMPION	X2
SERIE A CHAMPION	X2

International Stats

CAPS	GOALS
212	130

BIOGRAPHY

BORN	FEB 5, 1985
NATIONALITY	PORTUGUESE
STRONG FOOT	RIGHT
HEIGHT	1.87 M (6 FT 2 IN)
RETIRED	STILL PLAYING

In the same style as Pelé, Ronaldo just loves to score goals. Unlike Pelé, who started out as a 9 and dropped deeper as he got older, Ronaldo began life as a winger but gradually moved further forward, operating strictly as a goalscorer. But Cristiano Ronaldo is an original. There has never been anyone like him.

Ask any kid in a schoolyard or any adult on the street who is the best between Ronaldo and Messi, and you will never get the same answer. Since the early 2000s, football fans have been spoiled with world-class players, but Ronaldo and Messi have stood out above the rest.

Cristiano Ronaldo dos Santos Aveiro was born in a poor area of Funchal, the capital of the Portuguese island of Madeira. He was the fourth of four children, and times were so tough that his mother wasn't sure if they could afford to have a fourth child. Thankfully, she did, and a true world star was born.

Cristiano grew up sharing a bedroom with his three siblings. His mother worked two jobs, while his father, a struggling alcoholic, sometimes got shifts as a gardener. Times were extremely tough.

As you might suspect, Cristiano was a genius with a ball at his feet from a very young age. He was spotted at 12 by Sporting Lisbon, one of the biggest teams in

Portugal, and signed up for £1,500. Two years later, Cristiano's parents were called into his school and told that their kid didn't seem interested in schoolwork. It was true—he wasn't interested, as all he wanted to do was play football. Somehow, he persuaded his parents to let him drop out of school and concentrate solely on football.

Now, Cristiano could practise and train every waking hour, and that's just what he did. His work ethic* has always been tremendous, and it's carried on throughout his career. It's why he's still fitter than most 20-year-olds well into his late thirties. He's what you kids call a "monster"!

Growing up, his two favourite players were Ronaldo (the Brazilian one) and Ronaldinho, which isn't really surprising. If you put Ronaldo's (the Brazilian one!) goal-scoring and Ronaldinho's trickery into an oven and baked them together for a while, Cristiano Ronaldo would pop out! He's like a hybrid of their best qualities.

The tournament that Cristiano would grow up to dominate, the Champions League, was actually where he made his professional debut. He came on as a sub against Inter Milan in a game in August 2002 and instantly impressed. He was just 16!

He scored his first Sporting Lisbon goal a month later, and soon after, the world's best teams were chasing him. The two that came the closest were Manchester United and Arsenal, but United got there first. The rest, as they say, is history!

After just 25 games for Sporting, Cristiano signed for United in a £12 million deal that made him the most expensive teenager at the time. In his first season, he was more of an impact player, coming off the bench here and there and starting the odd game. He had immense skills and many tricks, but it was felt that he wouldn't last in the Premier League.

After winning the FA Cup in his first season, United hit a bit of a slump. They were building a new, young side, with Cristiano expected to be the main star. It took a few years, but soon, he was ripping it up in a three-pronged attack with Wayne Rooney and Carlos Tevez. United were exceptional.

Cristiano came into Euro 2004 as a young talent, but not the superstar he would become. Portugal were the host nation, and when they got to the final and met Greece, nobody in the world expected anything but a Portuguese victory. Greece shocked everyone, winning 1–0 and claiming the title. Ronaldo was devastated.

He took his anger out on opposition defences, and by 2007, United were back to their best. They won the league that year, then retained it the following season, with Cristiano scoring 42 goals! They also won the Champions League that year, and Cristiano claimed his first Ballon d'Or as well as the FIFA World Player of the Year award.

United won their third league in a row the following season, but they lost to Messi and Barcelona in the Champions League final.

After years of rumours, he finally signed for Real

Madrid in 2009 for a world-record £80 million fee, where he took the number 9 jersey. Madrid legend Raúl, who we'll cover later in the book, wore 7. Cristiano's first season ended trophyless, despite Madrid racking up 96 points, with Cristiano scoring 33 goals. Raúl retired at the end of that year, and Cristiano got his beloved number 7!

Cristiano struggled in the 2010 World Cup. Amazingly, people questioned if he could ever be considered a great if he didn't perform at the international level.

In his second season with Real, Cristiano scored 53 goals, helping the team lift the Copa del Rey, the first of many trophies he'd win in Madrid. He scored even more the following year (60) as Madrid won the league, yet he still finished behind Messi in the Ballon d'Or voting.

The Ballon d'Or judges couldn't ignore him at the end of the 2013–14 season, though. He scored 69 goals, including 17 in the Champions League as Madrid lifted the title. He won the Ballon d'Or again the following season.

On 12 September 2015, Cristiano became Real Madrid's all-time leading scorer when he netted for the 230th time. A year later, at Euro 2016 in France, he finally won his first international trophy as Portugal beat the host nation 1–0 in the final. Cristiano was injured during the final, but he carried Portugal to that point, and he celebrated like never before! He won his fourth Ballon d'Or at the end of the year.

Cristiano's two goals against Bayern in the quarterfinal

of the Champions League made him the first player in history to score 100 in the competition. In his last year with Madrid (2017), he won the league and the Champions League, again winning the Ballon d'Or.

He shocked everyone by leaving Real that summer, signing for Italian giants Juventus for £100 million, making him the most expensive signing in Serie A history and the most expensive player over the age of 30. In his first year, he won the Serie A's first-ever MVP award as he led the team to the league title. He won the league and the cup the following year before returning to Manchester United in 2021.

Things went well at the beginning of his second spell with United, and in his only full season, Cristiano finished as the club's top scorer. When Erik ten Hag took charge, everything turned sour, and Cristiano soon found himself on the bench a lot. He left on 22 November 2022, moving to the new Saudi Pro League, where he signed for Al Nassr.

Portugal were stunned by Morocco at the 2022 World Cup, getting knocked out in the quarterfinals. Still, Cristiano Ronaldo became the only man to have played in five separate World Cups, showing his unbelievable fitness. This was proven again in March 2023 when he earned his 197th cap for Portugal, making him the most-capped male player in history. His dedication to staying at the top of his game is undeniable.

Cristiano is still ripping it up in Saudi Arabia at 39, and he continues to perform for Portugal. He shows no signs of slowing down, so who knows how many records he'll hold by the time he finally hangs up his boots!

ROBERT
LEWANDOWSKI

Teams

DELTA WARSAW
2005
APPS – 17, GLS – 4
↓
ZNICZ PRUSZKÓW
2006–2008
APPS – 59, GLS – 36
↓
LECH POZNAŃ
2008–2010
APPS – 58, GLS – 32
↓
BORUSSIA DORTMUND
2010–2014
APPS – 131, GLS – 74
↓
BAYERN MUNICH
2014–2022
APPS – 253, GLS – 238
↓
BARCELONA
2022–
APPS – 69, GLS – 42

Trophy Cabinet

CHAMPIONS LEAGUE	X1
BUNDESLIGA CHAMPION	X10
LA LIGA CHAMPION	X1
FIFA CLUB WORLD CUP	X1
GERMAN SUPER CUP	X4
SPANISH SUPER CUP	X1

International Stats

CAPS	GOALS
152	83

BIOGRAPHY

BORN	AUG 21, 1988
NATIONALITY	POLISH
STRONG FOOT	RIGHT
HEIGHT	1.85M
RETIRED	STILL PLAYING

Much like Cristiano Ronaldo, Robert Lewandowski is one of those modern players who keeps himself in unbelievable shape. In fact, he is so ripped that one of his nicknames is "The Body"! His fitness has allowed him to play at the highest level all through his career, and at 35 (at the time of this book being written), he is still one of the best players in the world.

Robert Lewandowski was born in Warsaw, Poland, on 21 August 1988. He was raised in a Catholic home, where sports of all types were encouraged. Both of his parents loved anything athletic, and as soon as Robert showed early signs of his passion for football, his father began bringing him to watch local side Partyzant Leszno train. Robert was instantly obsessed, and he used to study and take notes of what the players were doing to improve their game.

Robert trained hard, and by the time he was 9, he was already on the radar of several professional clubs. He signed for Varsovia Warsaw, who were not exactly a top club, but he wanted to stay close to home. Varsovia's youth team's training ground was dusty and hard, but Robert didn't care. He was playing football every day, and that was all that mattered.

He spent seven years polishing his skills at Varsovia before signing for third division side Delta Warsaw. It was a huge move, but it was soon followed by tragedy when Robert's biggest fan and rock, his father, died. It hit Robert hard, and he hated that his dad would never get to see him one day play in the Ekstraklasa (Poland's top division).

It didn't take long for Robert to break into Delta's first team, and as soon as he did, he began scoring regularly. In his first two years, he was top scorer as the team got promoted at the end of both seasons. He was already one of the hottest prospects in European football.

Still a little raw, some of the bigger European sides decided to wait. In the end, he signed for Lech Poznań, one of the most popular clubs in Poland. His debut came in the UEFA Cup (now the Europa League) when he came on as a substitute and scored after a few minutes. Later that year (2008), he made his Poland debut, coming on as a sub and scoring once more!

Robert finished as the league's second-highest scorer in his first season and went one better the following year, finishing top. Lech Poznań also won the league that year, and Robert had the first of his many league winner's medals. He would go on to win many, many more.

Several clubs fought for his signature, but it was Jürgen Klopp and Borussia Dortmund who got him. He signed in time for the 2010–11 season, and by the end of the year, he had won the Bundesliga and finished with the Golden Boot, having scored 22 goals!

The summer of 2012 was memorable for Robert, as Poland were hosting the Euros. Poland were expected to do well, mainly because they had Lewandowski up front, and it started well. In the first game, he scored and got man of the match in a 1–1 draw with Greece, but Poland didn't perform to the best and crashed out in the group stage.

He was named captain of Poland the following year, and he scored his first international hat trick soon after. He continued to bang them in for Dortmund, winning a second league title in a row and reaching the Champions League final. Sadly, Dortmund lost the final to arch-rivals Bayern Munich.

In the final of the DFB-Pokal Cup, Dortmund got the better of Bayern, smashing them 5–2 as Robert helped himself to a hat trick. It was an incredible moment for Dortmund in the story of their heated rivalry with Bayern.

It was that very rivalry that caused so much hassle when, at the end of the 2013–14 season, Robert left Dortmund on a free to join Bayern.

Robert and Bayern won the league in his first season. Amazingly, he would go on to win another seven in a row as Bayern completely dominated German football. He was also top scorer in six of the eight seasons he spent in Munich.

One of his most memorable moments in a Bayern shirt (and in his whole career) came on 22 September 2015 in a game against Wolfsburg. With 59 minutes gone and Bayern 1–0 down, Pep Guardiola sent on his main striker. What followed is probably one of the most magical nine minutes in the history of football.

Robert Lewandowski scored five goals in eight minutes and 59 seconds, including the Bundesliga's fastest-ever hat trick, banging in three in just under four minutes.

At the 2016 Euros in France, Poland reached the quarterfinals for the first time in their history. Despite Robert scoring in a 1–1 draw with Portugal, he couldn't help the team from losing on penalties. It was devastating, but Poland and Robert could be proud of their efforts.

A year after the Euros, he scored his 50th goal for Poland, making him his country's all-time record scorer. He scored 16 goals in the 2018 World Cup qualifying campaign, which was a record, but Poland didn't perform well at the tournament, and they didn't get past the group stage.

Robert had become the most feared number 9 in world football. With two good feet, a great leap and immense power, he has always been dangerous. Now, with massive experience added to these strengths, he was unstoppable. In 2020, he won the Champions League with Bayern, scoring 15 goals along the way. It is clear that he would have won the Ballon d'Or that year only for the Covid-19 pandemic to interrupt the season and cancel the awards.

After eight trophy-filled seasons with Bayern, Robert wanted a new challenge and moved to Barcelona. The 45 million Euros Barca paid was a record transfer fee for Bayern. In his first game for Barca, he scored a hat trick against Viktoria Plzeň in the Champions League, and at the end of his first season, he won the league! He was also the league's top scorer!

Robert Lewandowski is still ripping it up at the time of this book being written, and at 35, he still has a few years left at the top. Who knows how far his story will go, but you can be sure that wherever his career takes him, there will be plenty of goals!

RONALDO
LUÍS NAZÁRIO DE LIMA

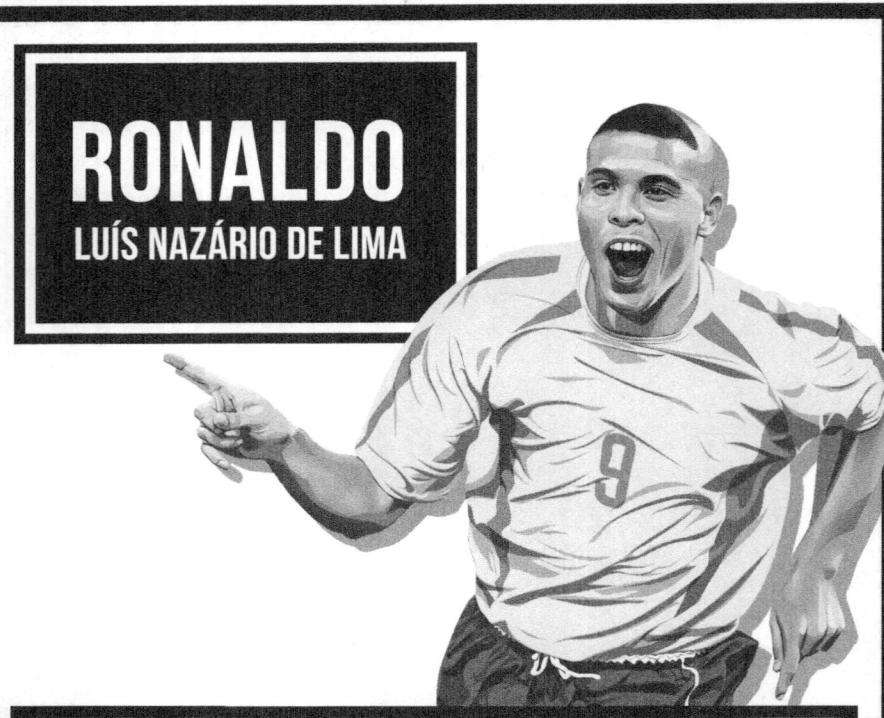

Teams

CRUZEIRO
1993–1994
APPS – 34, GLS – 34
↓
PSV
1994–1996
APPS – 46, GLS – 42
↓
BARCELONA
1996–1997
APPS – 37, GLS – 34
↓
INTER MILAN
1997–2002
APPS – 68, GLS – 49
↓
REAL MADRID
2002–2007
APPS – 127, GLS – 83
↓
AC MILAN
2007–2008
APPS – 20, GLS – 9
↓
CORINTHIANS
2009–2011
APPS – 52, GLS – 29

Trophy Cabinet

WORLD CUP	X2
COPA AMÉRICA	X2
BALLON D'OR	X2
LA LIGA CHAMPION	X2
UEFA SUPERCUP	X2
SPANISH CUP	X1

International Stats

CAPS	GOALS
98	62

BIOGRAPHY

BORN	SEPT 18, 1976
NATIONALITY	BRAZILIAN
STRONG FOOT	RIGHT
HEIGHT	1.83M
RETIRED	2011

Before Cristiano Ronaldo, there was, well... Ronaldo! Since the massive rise of Cristiano, some people have started to refer to the Brazilian Ronaldo as R9, using the first letter of his name and his favourite number to help separate them. To anyone who watched R9 in his prime, they were witnessing one of the most electric players in history.

The 1996–97 season, Ronaldo's only one with Barcelona, is often considered the greatest single season in any player's career. It wasn't as heavy on goals as some of Cristiano's, Messi's or Lewandowski's, but in that period, nobody (especially defenders) could get near Ronaldo. He was devastating, and several of his goals that year alone involved him beating six or seven players before slotting the ball home.

Ronaldo Luís Nazário de Lima was born on 18 September 1976, in Itaguaí, Rio de Janeiro. His family was poor, and when he was 11, his parents split up. A year later, Ronaldo had to drop out of school as his mother couldn't afford the fees. As bad as it was that he wouldn't be getting any more education, it gave Ronaldo more time to practise the sport he loved.

Like one of his idols, Pelé, Ronaldo learned his trade playing futsal, and his close control and dribbling skills on the football field were perfected on the tighter, compact surfaces. He joined his local team at 12, and in his first season, he scored 166 goals! Ronaldo was soon spotted by ex-Brazilian-player Jairzinho, who signed him for São Cristóvão. He was playing for their Under-20s when he was 15.

Ronaldo then signed for Cruzeiro. He had wanted to sign for his boyhood club, São Paulo, but they turned him down when he missed a training session. As it turned out, Ronaldo had only missed the session because he couldn't afford the bus fare. São Paulo's loss was Cruzeiro's gain!

By 17, Ronaldo was already unstoppable. In his first full season with Cruzeiro, he scored 20 goals in 21 games. In one game against Colo-Colo in the Supercopa Libertadores, he netted five. He finished as the tournament's top scorer, becoming the youngest player ever to do so.

Although he had only turned 17, Ronaldo was called up to the Brazilian squad for the 1994 World Cup in America. He was only brought in to gain experience, though, and he didn't play any minutes. Still, he got a taste for it, and he wanted more.

PSV Eindhoven signed him that same summer, and within a couple of years, he was on the move again as Barcelona won the race to sign the hottest property in world football. In his first season with PSV, he scored 30 goals, with most of them individual efforts where he left every defender chasing shadows.

Ronaldo's second season in Holland saw him struck down with the first of many injuries that would haunt him throughout his career. Despite this, he still managed 19 goals in 21 games, winning the Dutch Cup along the way. In his two years with PSV, he scored 54 goals in 58 appearances.

Barcelona paid nearly £20 million for Ronaldo, which was a world record by a long way. In his single season with Barca, he shredded defences for fun, with one of the greatest goals in history coming in a game against Compostela. Having picked the ball up in his own half and dodging several tackles, including a couple of clear fouls, Ronaldo carried the ball forward. A couple of feints and trademark stepovers later, and the ball was in the net.

At the end of the year, he was voted FIFA World Player of the Year, becoming the youngest player ever to win it. He was just 20.

After an argument over his contract, Barca shocked the world (and their furious fans!) when they sold Ronaldo to Inter Milan in 1997. Inter paid a world-record fee of £27 million, which was his buyout clause, but it was still seen as a bargain.

Ronaldo scored 25 goals in his first season with Inter, winning Serie A Footballer of the Year. He was now evolving, adding assists, free kicks and hold-up play to his game. He won FIFA World Player of the Year and the Ballon d'Or, and he was widely seen as the best player of his generation.

After lifting the UEFA Cup with Inter, Ronaldo went into the 1998 World Cup in France as the most feared attacker in world football. Brazil got to the final, but hours before the big game, Ronaldo suffered a seizure.

Despite this, he was still made to play the game, but he was only a shadow of himself, and France won 3–0. Ronaldo was devastated.

The following few years saw Ronaldo suffer some of the worst injuries imaginable. After buckling his knee at the start of the 1999–2000 season, he missed six months, but his troubles were far from over. Six minutes into his comeback game, Ronaldo's kneecap was shattered. In fact, one of the physios commented that his kneecap had exploded.

Following two major operations and more than a year on the sidelines, Ronaldo somehow returned for the 2002 World Cup. Almost everyone believed he was well past his best despite still being young. The injuries he'd suffered would have left many people in a wheelchair.

Ronaldo ripped the 2002 World Cup apart, forming a deadly partnership with Rivaldo and Ronaldinho, both of whom we will cover later in the book. Ronaldo won the Golden Boot, scoring eight goals as he helped Brazil lift the trophy. He was a world champion, and all those people who had thought he was past his best had to eat their words!

Following the World Cup, Ronaldo was the hottest property in football again. He signed for Real Madrid as one of the Galácticos*, and his jersey sale on his first day broke all records. His debut didn't come for several months after he picked up yet another injury, but he scored after 61 seconds when he finally did play and added a second before the end of the game.

One of the most magical moments in his career came at Old Trafford, the home of Manchester United. After destroying their defence for 67 minutes, Ronaldo was subbed off, only for the whole stadium (mostly United fans) to stand up and applaud.

After a successful spell with Madrid, Ronaldo moved to AC Milan and then Corinthians, but he was never close to his devastating best. He suffered endless injuries and weight problems before hanging up his boots in 2011. Since his retirement, he has moved upstairs and is currently the owner of Cruzeiro and Real Valladolid.

GERHARD MÜLLER

GERD

Teams

1861 NÖRDLINGEN
1963–1964
APPS – 31, GLS – 51
↓
BAYERN MUNICH
1964–1979
APPS – 453, GLS – 398
↓
FORT LAUDERDALE STRIKERS
1979–1981
APPS – 71, GLS – 38

Trophy Cabinet

WORLD CUP	X1
EUROS	X1
BALLON D'OR	X1
BUNDESLIGA CHAMPION	X4
GERMAN CUP WINNER	X4
INTERCONTINENTAL CUP	X2

International Stats

CAPS	GOALS
62	68

BIOGRAPHY

BORN	NOV 3, 1945
NATIONALITY	GERMAN
STRONG FOOT	RIGHT
HEIGHT	1.76M
RETIRED	1981

The man known as Der Bomber was one of the most clinical* strikers in history. A player who did nearly all of his work in the box, Gerd Müller was an old-school number 9 who seemed to be able to sniff out goal-scoring chances before they even happened. He is one of only nine players to have won the World Cup, Champions League and the Ballon d'Or, and his goals to games ratio is one of the best ever.

Gerd Müller was born in Nördlingen, Germany, just as World War II came to an end. With the country in ruins and now split into two, Gerd grew up in an awful time. His family had no money, and the only relief he found was when he was kicking a ball.

His youth career began with TSV 1861 Nördlingen, where he quickly earned a reputation as a goal poacher who would put his own safety at risk to put the ball in the net. He would often come off the training pitch with a bloodied nose or gashes, having thrown himself at the ball to get it over the line.

By the early 1960s, Gerd was the main player for Nördlingen's youth team, and in the 1962–63 season, he scored 180 goals. Yep, you read that correctly—he scored 180 goals in one season! He was soon spotted by Bayern Munich, who signed him when he was just 18.

As hard as it might be to imagine, given how massive

Bayern are today, in the mid-sixties, they were actually in the Regionalliga Süd, which was the second division. Bayern were in the process of building their first-ever great side, and they had future Germany legends Franz Beckenbauer and Sepp Maier in their team.

It took one season with these new stars for Bayern to get promoted (1965), and they soon began to dominate. By the end of the 1970s, Bayern would be known as one of the biggest and most glamorous clubs in Europe.

Gerd Müller wasn't built like a classic number 9 at the time. Back when centre forwards were usually six-foot-two and strong, Gerd was small and squat*. He was more like Sergio Aguero than Peter Crouch! Still, he could outjump just about everyone, and quite a lot of his goals were scored with his head.

After helping Bayern to promotion, Gerd soon caught the eye of the West German* national team. His debut came soon after the 1966 World Cup, in which the Germans had lost the final to England. Gerd's goal-scoring ratio for his country was even better than his for his club. He was devastating.

In Bayern's first season in the Bundesliga, they won the cup, which they would win again in 1967, '69 and '71 with Gerd in the team. They won the league in 1969 for only the second time in their history, and then four times in a row between 1971 and '74. From 1964 to 1978, Gerd Müller was Bayern's top scorer in each season!

At the 1970 World Cup, Gerd's first, he was immense. He scored in all three group games, including two hat tricks! In the quarterfinals, he helped West Germany* get revenge on England for the previous World Cup by beating them 3-2, with Gerd scoring the winner in extra time. Sadly, West Germany lost 4-3 in the semifinal to Italy. It is still seen as the greatest match in World Cup history.

Gerd Müller finished the 1970 World Cup with 10 goals. Most players dream of scoring just one at that level.

The next World Cup was to be held in West Germany, which really added to the pressure, but that is usually when German sides are at their best. They were actually drawn in a group with East Germany, and the East Germans shocked everyone when they finished top. West Germany still got through with their neighbours. After coming through another group, they met heavy favourites Holland in the final.

Holland had one of the best squads in history at the time, and their main star, Johan Cruyff, was a genius. Holland were seen as the entertainers, while West Germany were the hard-working, gritty team. Holland took the lead after just a few minutes, and they were expected to go on and thrash the Germans. Gerd Müller and his teammates had other plans, and they ground out a 2-1 win.

Gerd scored four goals at the 1974 World Cup, including the winner in the final. That meant he had 14 World Cup goals, making him the all-time leading scorer at the time. He also did it in just two World Cups, which is astonishing. Brazilian Ronaldo beat Gerd's record in 2006, but he needed more games to do it.

The same can be said for Gerd's international goal-scoring record. He scored 68 goals for Germany (in just 62 games!), a record that wasn't broken until Miroslav Klose beat it in 2014. Klose needed 137 games to do what Gerd Müller did in just 62!

Gerd retired from international football right after the '74 World Cup after falling out with the German Football Association. When everyone met up for the celebrations following West Germany's victory, only the board members were allowed to bring their wives. Gerd argued that this was unfair, as the players had done all the work, so their families should be allowed to party, too. He never played for his country again!

That summer had been unreal for Gerd. A few weeks before lifting the World Cup, he had helped Bayern win their first-ever European Cup (now the Champions League), when they beat Atlético Madrid in the final. Bayern and Gerd would go on to win it twice more over the next two years, making it three in a row.

He spent a couple of years in the MLS before retiring in 1981. Soon after leaving football, Gerd began struggling with alcoholism. Through the help of his old teammates and his family, he got healthy again, and he spent the rest of his life as one of Bayern Munich's most popular ambassadors.

Gerd Müller died in 2021, but he will always be remembered as one of the most clinical finishers in history.

FERENC PUSKÁS

Teams

BUDAPEST HONVÉD
1943–1956
APPS – 350, GLS – 358

↓

REAL MADRID
1958–1966
APPS – 180, GLS – 156

Trophy Cabinet

OLYMPIC GOLD MEDAL	X1
LA LIGA CHAMPION	X5
SPANISH CUP	X1
HUNGARIAN CHAMPION	X5
EUROPEAN CHAMPION CLUBS' CUP	X3

International Stats

CAPS	GOALS
89	84

BIOGRAPHY

BORN	APRIL 1, 1927
NATIONALITY	HUNGARIAN
STRONG FOOT	LEFT FOOT
HEIGHT	1.72M
RETIRED	1966

Around the time Pelé was breaking into the Brazil team in the late 1950s, another player was already tearing it up across the Atlantic Ocean. Brazil were the team to watch in the '60s and '70s, but before them, Hungary were the first entertainers. Before Ferenc Puskás and his silky teammates, skills such as drag backs and flicks had never been seen before.

That Hungary team of the '50s were a lot like the Holland team of the '70s—they played the best football in the world at the time, yet they just missed out on the biggest prize.

One cold November day in 1952, Hungary walked out onto the Wembley pitch to face an England team that had yet to lose an international home game. As Ferenc Puskás warmed up, one England player was apparently overheard saying, "Who is this tubby guy?" before nudging his teammate and laughing. The England team believed they were about to stroll to victory, but 90 minutes later, they had lost 6–3 to Hungary's Golden Team, and the 105,000 fans in the stadium had witnessed skills they'd never known existed.

This is one of the more popular stories about Ferenc Puskás, but there are many more. He changed the way football was played, and he did it with electrifying skill and a left foot like a magic wand.

Born and raised in Budapest, Hungary, Ferenc was the son of a pro football player and soon-to-be coach. His dad was a good player in his day, but his son is often called one of the greatest forwards in history.

Ferenc was a child prodigy who came along around the time that Hungary seemed to be producing one future legend after another. He grew up watching local team Kispest Honvéd train, as his father used to bring him, and it wasn't long before the scouts there signed him up on youth terms.

After impressing right away, Ferenc was pushed up through the ranks, and as soon as he turned 17, he was in the first team. Within weeks, he was a fan favourite due to his powerful shot, tricks and his ability to score from angles that never seemed possible. In one game against Gyor, Ferenc scored seven in an 11–3 victory!

In 1949, three years before that famous "Match of the Century" against England, Kispest Honvéd were taken over by the Hungarian Ministry of Defence. Under the new military rule, all of the players had to be given an army rank. Ferenc was made a major, and this would end up becoming part of his famous nickname, "The Galloping Major"!

In a move that would make PSG look like casual spenders, Honvéd took all the country's best Hungarian players in the league and forced them to sign for the team! All the other clubs lost out, but Honvéd became one of the best sides in Europe overnight! Future legends Zoltán Czibor and Sándor Kocsis (and many more) joined up with Puskás, forming one of the most devastating attacks in world football. Kocsis would go on to score 11 goals at the 1954 World Cup!

The Hungarian national team of the era became known as the Golden Team or the Mighty Magyars. They went on a fantastic 31 game unbeaten run that included victory at the 1952 Olympic Games (Puskás scored in the final), and two massive demolitions of England (the second game ended 7–1!). Sadly, the game that finished their streak was the World Cup final!

That 1954 World Cup should have been Hungary's crowning moment. They smashed everyone they faced, including Brazil, who they beat 4–2 in the semifinal. Amazingly, they had already demolished Germany 8–3 in the group stage earlier in the tournament before facing them again in the final. Unfortunately, Puskás picked up an injury and didn't return until the final. He still played the game (and scored twice) despite having a hairline fracture in his leg.

Germany stunned the world by winning 3–2, but the final has always been surrounded by controversy, as Germany were given one decision after another.

Two years later, Hungary erupted in civil war, and Ferenc and most of the Golden Team defected* to Spain. He joined Real Madrid and quickly formed an unstoppable partnership with Alfredo Di Stéfano (we will cover him later in the book!). In his first season with Madrid, Puskás scored four hat tricks, and in his first six seasons, he scored 20 or more goals every year, winning the Pichichi* in four of them.

In his eight seasons with Madrid, he won the league five times and the European Cup three times. He scored 156 goals in 180 games, with a career total of 600 goals in 620 games. Amazingly, after gaining citizenship in 1961, he actually played for Spain four times despite his long career as a Hungarian player!

One of his most magical games for Madrid saw him net four in the 1960 European Cup final as Madrid smashed Eintracht Frankfurt 7–3! His strike partner Alfredo Di Stéfano also scored a hat trick!

Ferenc retired in 1966 as a Hungarian and Real Madrid legend before moving into management. In 2002, the national stadium in Budapest was named after him. He passed away a few years later, but he must have been so proud to see his name on the stadium where he played so many magical games!

LIONEL MESSI

Teams

BARCELONA
2004–2021
APPS – 520, GLS – 474

↓

PARIS SAINT-GERMAIN
2021–2023
APPS – 58, GLS – 22

↓

INTER MIAMI
2023–
APPS – 18, GLS – 13

Trophy Cabinet

WORLD CUP	X1
COPA AMÉRICA	X2
BALLON D'OR	X8
LA LIGA CHAMPION	X10
SPANISH CUP	X7
FRENCH CHAMPION	X2

International Stats

CAPS	GOALS
187	109

BIOGRAPHY

BORN	JUNE 24, 1987
NATIONALITY	ARGENTINIAN
STRONG FOOT	LEFT
HEIGHT	1.7M
RETIRED	STILL PLAYING

When it comes to deciding who is the greatest modern-day player, the debate usually boils down to two players—Lionel Messi and Cristiano Ronaldo. Most pundits* and ex-players seem to pick Messi, with an awful lot of them going so far as to say he's the greatest ever.

Watching Messi in a game or looking up his highlight reels on YouTube makes it hard to argue against him being the GOAT. There has been nobody like him, with the closest in style being his fellow Argentinian legend, Diego Maradona. Some people used to claim that Messi could never be the GOAT as he hadn't won a World Cup. Well, that all changed in 2023, as Messi captained his nation to the biggest prize in football.

Lionel Messi was born on 24 June 1987 in Rosario, Santa Fe, Argentina. He was the third of four kids in a football-crazy family, and his father, Jorge, was obsessed with the game. Two of his cousins, Maximiliano and Emanuel Biancucchi, both went on to have successful professional football careers.

At 4, little Leo joined his local team, Grandoli, where his father was a coach. Leo has since said that his first hero was his grandmother, Celia, who brought him to most of his early games. She was his biggest fan. When she died, Leo was only 11, and it crushed him. Even today, when he does his fingers-to-the-sky celebration, he's remembering Celia.

A couple of years after joining Grandoli, Leo moved to his boyhood club, Newell's Old Boys. He was 6, yet his coaches could already tell they had a phenom on their books. There was one problem—Leo was tiny. And it wasn't just his height that was an issue, either. As a kid, Leo struggled to gain weight, and he always seemed too bony to take a tackle. When his coaches watched the much bigger defenders bouncing off the kid when he went on a run, they couldn't understand it. He seemed to be made of granite.

Lionel Messi has always had a low centre of gravity, and his core strength is unreal. His size has never been a problem for him on the pitch, and it only ever seemed to be an issue for a few coaches and scouts who couldn't see past it. They just took one look at him and said, "Nah, sorry, kid, but you're too small."

Things got worse for Leo when he was diagnosed with a hormone deficiency* at the age of 10. With the treatment costing far too much for his family to afford, he was told that his dream of being a pro footballer would probably never happen. Leo was heartbroken. You have to remember that this was one year before his grandmother passed away, so Leo had to be extremely mentally tough to get through those couple of years.

Newell's Old Boys then agreed to pay for the treatment, only to pull out of the deal a few weeks later. They didn't think Leo was worth the risk! River Plate then came in for him. One of Leo's heroes, Pablo Aimar, played there, so he was delighted. Following a trial, River somehow rejected him, thinking he wasn't good enough!

Some of his relatives lived in Catalonia, the home of Barcelona, and they managed to get him a trial. The family travelled to Spain, and after a few minutes on the training pitch, Leo was signed. Barca also agreed to pay for his medical treatment. In 2001, Lionel Messi became a Barcelona youth player, and the rest, as they say, is history!

By the following year, the once shy and quiet Leo was making friends in La Masia, the famous Barcelona youth academy. He started to make friends, becoming very close with Cesc Fàbregas and Gerard Piqué. When his growth hormone therapy finished, Leo was 14, and he was now the star player in the Baby Dream Team*!

He rose rapidly through the ranks and made his senior debut at 17. Soon after, he became La Liga's youngest goalscorer, as he easily slotted into a team with Ronaldinho and Samuel Eto'o. After a few starts and plenty of sub appearances in his first season, Barca won the league. Leo had a taste for winning, and he wanted more.

He helped Argentina win the 2005 FIFA World Youth Championships and then made his senior debut that same year. Instantly, he was compared to Diego Maradona, which is a pressure that had crushed many up-and-coming Argentinian players in the past.

He had his first taste of World Cup football in 2006, becoming Argentina's youngest player at that level. They crashed out in the quarterfinals, but Leo's career was only getting started. That summer, he had helped Barcelona to the Champions League final, only to miss the 2–1 win over Arsenal through injury. Still, he was a Champions League winner!

He led Argentina to gold at the 2008 Summer Olympics. It wasn't the World Cup, but it was a start.

When Pep Guardiola took over as Barca manager, everything came together for Leo. He had a manager who believed he was the best player in the world, and he wanted to build the team around him. He was played in a new false 9 role, and he flourished*. The first time he played there, Barca thumped arch-rivals Real Madrid 6–2 at the Bernabéu. It was Barca's biggest-ever win at Real's home.

The 2009 season was like nothing ever seen before. Barcelona won the sextuple*, cleaning house as they won every trophy available. Leo also claimed the Ballon d'Or and the FIFA World Player of the Year award. Several more would follow as Lionel Messi became widely known as the greatest player on the planet.

That year also saw the arrival of Cristiano Ronaldo in Spain, and one of football's greatest rivalries really took off!

After being named Argentina captain in 2011, Leo went on a run of final losses with his country that caused him to retire from international football in 2016. Argentina lost to Germany in the 2014 World Cup final and twice to Chile in the Copa América final.

Thankfully for Argentina, he came out of international retirement a couple of years later.

Leo continued to smash records, including a ridiculous individual season in 2011–12, when he scored 73 goals and provided 29 assists. He won the Ballon d'Or, of course! It's hard to imagine that he was still just 24!

He became Barca's record scorer in 2014 and then won another treble the following year. He continued to count off leagues, cups and Ballon d'Ors, winning his sixth of the latter in 2019.

His Barca career came to a shock end in 2021 when the team fell into financial trouble and had to sell him. He joined PSG, where two leagues in two years followed, but his best moment in football was yet to come.

Lionel Messi finally lifted the World Cup in the summer of 2023, scoring seven goals and winning a record second Golden Ball along the way. He broke the record for most games played at a World Cup (26) and a record 8th Ballon d'Or. To those who used to claim that he couldn't be the best until he won a World Cup, the argument was over.

Leo is still playing at the time of this book being written, and he continues to boss it in the MLS. His international career shows no sign of stopping, and he will be 39 when the next World Cup rolls around. Who wouldn't be surprised if he won it again?

RONALDINHO GAÚCHO

Teams

GRÊMIO
1998–2001
APPS – 89, GLS – 47
↓
PARIS SAINT-GERMAIN
2001–2003
APPS – 55, GLS – 17
↓
BARCELONA
2003–2008
APPS – 145, GLS – 70
↓
AC MILAN
2008–2011
APPS – 76, GLS – 20
↓
FLAMENGO
2011–2012
APPS – 56, GLS – 23
↓
ATLÉTICO MINEIRO
2012–2014
APPS – 58, GLS – 20
↓
QUERÉTARO
2014–2015
APPS – 25, GLS – 8
↓
FLUMINENSE
2015
APPS – 7, GLS – 0

Trophy Cabinet

WORLD CUP	X1
COPA AMÉRICA	X1
BALLON D'OR	X1
CHAMPIONS LEAGUE	X1
LA LIGA CHAMPION	X2
SERIE A CHAMPION	X1

International Stats

CAPS	GOALS
97	33

BIOGRAPHY

BORN	MARCH 21, 1980
NATIONALITY	BRAZILIAN
STRONG FOOT	RIGHT
HEIGHT	1.82M
RETIRED	2018

Much like his international teammate Ronaldo (R9), Ronaldinho seemed to shine brightly for much too short a period. His bad habits and laid-back attitude meant that he was only in his prime for a handful of seasons, but in that time, he left a mark like nobody else before or after him.

He is possibly the greatest dribbler in history, although Lionel Messi and Diego Maradona fans might disagree. At the very least, Ronaldinho was the most entertaining player in history. He could do things with a ball that other players can't even dream up. He was a showboat but in the most devastating way imaginable.

Born in Porto Alegre, Rio Grande do Sul, on 21 March 1980, Ronaldo de Assis Moreira grew up with little. Much like Leo Messi, Ronaldinho's family was obsessed with football. His older brother Roberto was a brilliant player, and he was signed by Grêmio when Ronaldinho was just a boy. The club moved the family to a much nicer neighbourhood, buying them a new house as part of Roberto's deal.

Sadly, Roberto's career was cut short by a horrific injury, and soon after, Ronaldinho's father died in a freak accident when he slipped by the pool and hit his head.

Again, like Messi, Ronaldinho was small for his age. It

was his height that earned him the name we all know today—Ronaldinho. Ronald was his first name, and "inho" means small. His friends put the two together, and the legend was born!

Ronaldinho preferred futsal and beach soccer at first, where winning sometimes takes a back seat to showboating and skills. It's more entertaining, and Ronaldinho has always been an entertainer.

He made the local newspapers at 13 when he scored all 23 goals in a 23–0 win for his local side. Much like his childhood idols, Rivellino, Maradona and Romário (he's covered soon!), Ronaldinho loved to dribble, score and be the standout player on the pitch. His two modern-day favourite players, Ronaldo (R9) and Rivaldo, became his teammates years later!

Ronaldinho was part of the Brazilian Under-17 team that won the World Championship in 1997. He had already signed with Grêmio, but after that, Europe's biggest teams were circling. Arsenal came very close to signing him but work permit* issues ruined the deal. We can only dream about how well he would have slotted into a team with Thierry Henry and Dennis Bergkamp!

In the end, PSG signed him for €5 million.

Ronaldinho won his first cap for Brazil in 1999, and he was part of the squad that won that year's Copa América. He was making a name for himself as the type of player who only scored worldies*, but some people questioned his dedication to the game. This would follow him throughout his career, even when winning World Cups and Champion Leagues.

By the 2001-02 season, he was starting to break into the PSG first team. In the second half of the season, he ignited, shredding defence after defence, his mazy runs and classy finishing amazing everyone who watched. He was given the number 10 jersey the following year, and although he wasn't at his best that season, he showed glimpses of his genius.

That summer, he starred for Brazil as they won the 2002 World Cup. His partnership with Ronaldo and Rivaldo was devastating, and Ronaldinho scored one of the goals of the tournament in the quarterfinal win over England when he lobbed the keeper with a 45-yard free kick. He missed the semi through suspension but returned for the final as Brazil lifted the trophy.

In 2003, Barcelona went all out to sign a superstar. The team had fallen dramatically, finishing outside the top four on several occasions. They missed out on Thierry Henry and David Beckham, so they signed Ronaldinho. It turned out to be one of the greatest signings in history.

A year after he signed, Barca hadn't just improved; they were back to their best. They won the league, with Ronaldinho as the main man, and most of his teammates credit him for single-handedly making Barcelona great again. His stick-and-twist goal against Chelsea in the Champions League was like nothing seen before or after. If you haven't seen it, look it up!

On 1 May 2005, Ronaldinho set up 17-year-old Lionel Messi for his first-ever Barcelona goal! The torch would be passed a few years later.

He finished that season with the league title, the Ballon d'Or, and his second FIFA World Player of the Year award in a row. One of his most memorable moments actually came at the home of Real Madrid, Barca's hated rivals. After ripping Real apart the entire game, Ronaldinho went on another mazy run before slotting the ball past Iker Casillas. Instead of booing, the Real fans stood up and applauded. This had only ever happened once before for a Barca player at the Bernabéu when Diego Maradona was given a standing ovation.

The 2005–06 season is often seen as Ronaldinho's greatest. He won the Champions League—Barca's first in 14 years—and the La Liga title. He finished with 26 goals and a bunch of assists, with just about all of his goals highlight reel stuff.

By 2008, Ronaldinho's injuries had started to pile up, and he began partying more. His fitness suffered, and at the end of the season, Barcelona moved him on. He signed for AC Milan for €25 million, picking the number 80 jersey, as Clarence Seedorf had the 10.

Ronaldinho showed flashes of his brilliance, and he even won Milan's Player of the Year in his second season and then the Serie A in 2011. But that championship-winning season ended up being his last, and he missed a lot of it through injury. After Milan, Ronaldinho played for a few Brazilian clubs, winning the 2013 Copa Libertadores with Atlético Mineiro.

Ronaldinho retired from football in 2018, having won

pretty much everything there was to win. Still, one question will always remain: Just how good could he have been if he'd stayed fit? Who knows. But one thing is certain. For those few years when he was in his prime, there was nobody better than Ronaldinho.

EUSÉBIO
DA SILVA FERREIRA

THE BLACK PANTHER

Teams

SPORTING LOURENÇO MARQUES
1957–1960
APPS – 42, GLS – 77
↓
BENFICA
1961–1975
APPS – 301, GLS – 317
↓
BOSTON MINUTEMEN
1975
APPS – 7, GLS – 2
↓
MONTERREY
1975
APPS – 10, GLS – 1
↓
TORONTO METROS-CROATIA
1975–1976
APPS – 21, GLS – 16
↓
BEIRA-MAR
1976
APPS – 12, GLS – 3
↓
LAS VEGAS QUICKSILVERS
1976–1977
APPS – 17, GLS – 2
↓
UNIÃO DE TOMAR
1977–1978
APPS – 12, GLS – 3

Trophy Cabinet

BALLON D'OR	X1
PORTUGUESE CHAMPION	X11
PORTUGUESE CUP	X5
EUROPEAN CHAMPION CLUBS' CUP	X1

International Stats

CAPS	GOALS
64	41

BIOGRAPHY

BORN	JAN 25, 1942
NATIONALITY	PORTUGESE
STRONG FOOT	RIGHT
HEIGHT	1.75M
RETIRED	1979

As one of the first black players to represent Portugal, Eusébio was a trailblazer* in a lot of ways. He constantly dealt with racism, especially when Portugal were on tour, but he never let it hold him back. In fact, he used it to spur him on, becoming Benfica's most beloved player in the club's history.

A dynamic, powerful and two-footed forward, Eusébio terrorised defences all over the world. His goals to games ratio was unreal, but he was also a creator, often dropping deep and threading his teammates through. Another legend, Alfredo Di Stéfano, once said that Eusébio was the best of the lot—the true GOAT.

Eusébio da Silva Ferreira was born in Mozambique, Africa, and not Portugal. But Mozambique was a Portuguese colony, and his father was Portuguese. He was the fourth of five children, and like a lot of players in this book, he grew up in a football-mad household.

His family didn't have much money, and Eusébio often played barefoot. His father, who was a lifelong Benfica fan, died when Eusébio was just 8. It hit him hard, and what little money the family had coming in was gone. Eusébio's mother raised the kids on her own.

His first youth team was called Os Brasileiros (The Brazilians), and they played in yellow shirts and blue shorts. As mentioned earlier, Brazil were the first team in world football to become widely popular, and Mozambique in the 1950s was no different. This was when Pelé was just breaking into the Brazil team, and every kid wanted to be just like him!

Because of Mozambique's connection with Portugal, most of the top Portuguese clubs had feeder teams* there, including Eusébio's boyhood team, Benfica. Unfortunately, they didn't show much of an interest in him as a kid, but Sporting Lisbon did. Eusébio and some of his pals were given a trial, with most of them wearing boots for the first time.

Sporting signed him and quickly promoted him to their Mozambique-based team, Sporting Clube de Lourenço Marques. Eusébio played three seasons with them, scoring 77 goals in 42 games! When he turned 18, it was time to move to Lisbon.

But things took a turn when Eusébio landed in Portugal. His beloved Benfica were interested, but Sporting said they would block any transfer if he didn't sign for them. They had a verbal agreement* and wanted Eusébio to follow through. He held out for his dream move, though, risking everything to sign for Benfica. Because of all the legal stuff, he had to wait a year to play for his new team, but it was worth the wait!

A 19-year-old Eusébio made his Benfica debut on 1 June 1961, scoring in a 4–1 loss. He made his international debut a few months later, scoring again in another loss. Strangely, though, he didn't make that Benfica debut until the end of the season, so he only played a couple of times before the teams broke for the summer!

He started his first full season on fire, banging in 12 goals in his opening 17 games and helping Benfica to the Taça de Portugal*. He scored two in the final, and if he hadn't already won over the Benfica fans, he certainly did a couple of weeks later when he scored another two in the European Cup final! Benfica beat Real Madrid 5–3.

The previous year, Benfica had also won the European Cup, lifting it for the first time. They beat Barcelona in the final, becoming the first team apart from Real Madrid to win the competition. As you will see in the next biography, Real won the first five European Cups before they were finally stopped!

Benfica and Eusébio would reach three more European Cup finals in the 1960s, losing them all. The 1967–68 final is still remembered as one of the greatest, as a George Best-inspired Manchester United lifted the trophy for the first time.

You'll read all about Best later in the book!

By the 1966 World Cup in England, Eusébio was one of the most feared strikers in the world. In fact, it was basically between him and Pelé. He lived up to his reputation in the tournament, scoring in the group wins over Bulgaria and holders Brazil. He netted two in that 3–1 win over Brazil.

In what would have been the biggest shock in World Cup history, Portugal went 3–0 down after 25 minutes to unheard-of North Korea. Just about all of the North

Korean players had other jobs, and they only played part-time. Thankfully for Portugal, Eusébio stepped up, pulling a goal back on 27 minutes. He then slotted home a penalty just before half-time to give the team hope.

In the second half, he picked up where he had left off, scoring the equaliser on 56 before giving Portugal the lead for the first time three minutes later. José Augusto made it 5–3, and Portugal had scraped through.

Eusébio scored again in the semifinal against England, but two Bobby Charlton goals gave the hosts the win. Portugal were out, but Eusébio's goal in a 2–1 win over the Soviet Union* in the third-place playoff brought his total to nine for the tournament, winning him the Golden Boot.

Eusébio would never play in another World Cup, but his tally was already one of the highest. As for his club side, he was a relentless winner. Benfica won seven leagues in the 1960s and began the 1970s with three in a row. Eusébio won the Ballon d'Or in 1965 and was the runner-up twice. He was also the first-ever winner of the Golden Shoe, given to the top scorer of all the European leagues. He won it again five years later.

A lifelong Benfica fan, Eusébio stayed at the team he adored for most of his career. In his time there, he scored a whopping 473 goals in just 440 matches. He is still regarded as Benfica's greatest-ever player, and it's safe to say that will never change.

After Portugal, he spent some time in the MLS, winning the 1976 Soccer Bowl. He died in 2014 at the age of 71, with the whole of Portugal and world football paying their respects. A true legend.

ALFREDO DI STÉFANO

TEAMS

RIVER PLATE
1945–1949
APPS – 66, GLS – 49
↓
HURACÁN (LOAN)
1945–1946
APPS – 25, GLS – 10
↓
MILLONARIOS
1949–1953
APPS – 101, GLS – 90
↓
REAL MADRID
1953–1964
APPS – 282, GLS – 216
↓
ESPANYOL
1964–1966
APPS – 47, GLS – 11

TROPHY CABINET

COPA AMÉRICA	X1
BALLON D'OR	X2
LA LIGA CHAMPION	X8
SPANISH CUP	X1
COLOMBIAN CHAMPION	X3
ARGENTINIAN CHAMPION	X2

INTERNATIONAL STATS

CAPS	GOALS
41	29

BIOGRAPHY

BORN	JULY 4, 1926
NATIONALITY	ARGENTINIAN
STRONG FOOT	RIGHT
HEIGHT	1.78M
RETIRED	1966

It would be impossible to have a list of legends without including the man who not only won the first five European Cups but scored in every one of the finals. He was one of the first foreign imports to become a star at Real Madrid, and he opened the door for many more to follow, including Ferenc Puskás, who became Di Stéfano's deadly strike partner for several years!

Born on 4 July 1926 in Buenos Aires, Argentina, Alfredo Di Stéfano saw professional football up close from an early age. His father was a superb defender who played for River Plate, one of the biggest clubs in Argentina. Alfredo used to love nothing more than going to watch his father play, but when a horrific knee injury ended Alfredo Sr's career early, that all stopped.

Young Alfredo found himself playing (and falling in love with) street football. This was where he learned how to take a tackle, control the ball in tight spaces and score into smaller nets. When his father found work in the countryside, the family were forced to move away from the city. At first, Alfredo Jnr was devastated, but he soon discovered organised football, and he quickly discovered that he had a gift.

In between playing for his new youth team, he had to work with his father. Times were tough, and everyone in the family had to do their share. His father could see his son's talent, though, and he sent a telegram* to his old club, River Plate, telling them they needed to take a look. They offered Alfredo Jnr a trial, and within weeks, he was signed.

He broke into the first team at 19, playing a few games here and there as River won the league. Still, he felt like he hadn't done much, and he wanted to gain more first team experience. River agreed and allowed him to go out on loan to relegation battlers Huracán.

A left-footed player who could switch from a number 9 to either wing or even drop deeper as a number 10, Di Stéfano was deadly. Regarded as one of the best dribblers of all time, he was quick and had great vision, causing nightmares for defences every time he stepped onto the field.

This all became clear at Huracán, where he was now getting a run of games. He helped the team to a shock top-half finish in his only season with them, scoring several goals as he became their star man. In one game against his parent club* River, he scored the quickest goal in the history of the Argentinian league, netting after just 10 seconds!

Huracán wanted to keep him, but River recalled him after a year. He was instantly given a starting role, and he scored 27 goals as River won the league. But things were about to turn sour, and soon after, Di Stéfano and a few other top players went on strike. At the time, the Argentinian league was one of the worst for players' rights, and most barely earned enough to pay the bills.

The strike didn't work, and the league almost

collapsed. Di Stéfano and most of the country's top talent left for a better life. At the time, the Columbian league was one of the richest in the world. If you think of the Saudi Pro League today, it was a little like that, with players from all over Europe and South America moving to Colombian clubs for huge wages! Di Stéfano did the same, signing for Millonarios in 1949.

He spent four years in Columbia, winning the league three times and the cup once. He also scored 90 goals in 101 games, with Millonarios becoming famous all over the world. Clubs in Europe wanted to organise friendlies, as they had heard about this collection of world stars all playing for one team.

Real Madrid invited Millonarios for a friendly tournament in the summer of 1953, expecting the rumours of how good they were not to be true. Madrid were trying to build the best team in Europe, and they wanted to put these Columbian wannabes in their place! It didn't work, as Di Stéfano and his team won the tournament. By the time he had landed back in Columbia, Di Stéfano had telegrams from both Real and Barcelona, with both teams wanting to sign him.

In the end, Real won out on his signature and would soon go on the most dominant run in the history of European club football. To this day, Barca hate that it could have been them who dominated if only Di Stéfano had chosen the Camp Nou over the Bernabéu!

He was 27 when he signed for Real, but he soon made up for lost time. In his first season, he won the league, Madrid's first in two decades. He won the Pichichi, and then helped Madrid retain the league the following year. This is important as the next season would be the first-ever European Cup, meaning Real Madrid were the first Spanish team to play in it. Before it became the Champions League, only the league winners from each country qualified.

That same season, Di Stéfano just missed out on the first-ever Ballon d'Or, losing by three votes to English legend Stanley Matthews.

Madrid lifted the inaugural* European Cup, beating French side Reims 4–3 in the final. Di Stéfano scored one of the goals. He won the Ballon d'Or that year!

In the 1956–57 season, a footballing miracle occurred when Real Madrid went on what has to be considered as one of the most incredible winning runs in any sport. They won every home game in La Liga from midway through the 1956–57 season until midway through the 1965–66 season! That's nearly a decade of home wins (not even a draw!) and a total of 121 on the trot until they were stopped!

As mentioned, Real also won the first five European Cups, beating Fiorentina in the second, then AC Milan, Reims (again) and finally Eintracht Frankfurt in 1960. That last one was a 7–3 victory, with Di Stéfano scoring a hat trick while Puskás, as we mentioned, netted four!

As an international, Alfredo Di Stéfano played for three different countries! He played for Argentina six times, scoring six, but he played more times for Spain, earning 31 caps and scoring 23 goals. He also played a few games for Columbia!

He moved to Espanyol in his late thirties and played there for a couple of years, but he was never the same. Many years of management followed, with spells at clubs such as Valencia, Boca Juniors and Juventus. He won a few leagues as a manager, including the 1970–71 La Liga title with Valencia.

His partnership with Puskás didn't happen until 1958, when Di Stéfano was 34, but they had several seasons where they were the most dangerous partnership in world football. Some would say it was the best partnership ever. Whatever the case may be, Alfredo Di Stéfano is, without a doubt, one of the best forwards in the history of the game.

LUÍS FIGO

Teams

SPORTING CP
1989–1995
APPS – 129, GLS – 16
↓
BARCELONA
1995–2000
APPS – 172, GLS – 30
↓
REAL MADRID
2000–2005
APPS – 164, GLS – 38
↓
INTER MILAN
2005–2009
APPS – 105, GLS – 9

Trophy Cabinet

BALLON D'OR	X1
CHAMPIONS LEAGUE	X1
LA LIGA CHAMPION	X4
SERIE A CHAMPION	X4
UEFA SUPERCUP	X2
SPANISH CUP	X2

International Stats

CAPS	GOALS
127	32

BIOGRAPHY

BORN	NOV 4, 1972
NATIONALITY	PORTUGESE
STRONG FOOT	RIGHT
HEIGHT	1.8M
RETIRED	2009

A tricky winger with an eye for a goal, Luís Figo was one of the most feared players of his generation. His move from Barcelona to Real Madrid has to be the most controversial of all time, and the hatred it brought afterwards was horrible. Still, Figo rose above it all, and he went on to be one of the jewels in the Galácticos team of the early 2000s.

Born Luís Filipe Madeira Caeiro Figo on 4 November 1972, Luís grew up in Cova da Piedade, a working-class neighbourhood. He learned his trade playing futsal, which had spread from Brazil to countries like Portugal and Spain. Luís was an outstanding player, even as a kid.

He was first spotted by Sporting Lisbon, who signed him to a youth contract when he was 12. He rose through the ranks but was only seen as a good player and not a future Ballon d'Or winner! Unlike some of the players on this list, Luís Figo's rise wasn't explosive, and he sort of edged his way to the top. Once he was there, though, he shone just as brightly as anyone else!

After coming up through the youth sides, Luís earned his place in the senior team and made his debut on 1 April 1990 against Maritimo. He was eased into the first team over the next couple of seasons, scoring a handful of goals and impressing with his tricks and dribbling.

Unlike a lot of wingers, Luís Figo wasn't small. He was pretty tall, actually, and stocky, too. But he was quick, sharp and explosive. He could play with both feet, and his finishing was as good as any number 9.

He made his Portugal debut in 1991, following his starring role with Portugal's golden generation at the FIFA Under-20 World Championships, which Portugal won. Other future stars such as Rui Costa and João Pinto had come through with him, and big things were expected of Portugal over the next decade or so.

In his final season with Sporting, he won the Portuguese Cup, and some of Europe's top teams began to make bids. Surprisingly, it wasn't a crazy bidding war, and there were a few notable big clubs who didn't try to sign him. Barcelona were interested, though, and they got him at the shockingly low price of £2.25 million!

If people hadn't been convinced Figo was good enough at Sporting, they were soon shown how wrong they were once he started playing for Barca. By the 1996–97 season, Luís Figo was one of the best players in the world, and his link-up play with Ronaldo (R9) was unstoppable. They won the European Cup Winners' Cup that year, and when Ronaldo left for Inter Milan, Figo stepped up as the main man.

He formed another devastating partnership, this time with Patrick Kluivert and Rivaldo. Together, they won two La Liga titles in a row.

The summer of 2000 saw possibly the most controversial transfer in football history when

Barcelona came out of nowhere to pay Figo's buyout clause (£62 million). Figo was on the verge of winning the Ballon d'Or, and he was widely seen as the best player in the world at the time. Barca's biggest rivals signing him meant only one thing—war!

In truth, Figo hadn't wanted to leave, but the bid was accepted, and he was left with no choice. All loyalty he felt toward the Barca fans would disappear the first time he stepped onto the pitch against them!

That same summer, at Euro 2000, all eyes were on him. He was known as the best, and people wanted to see if Portugal's Golden Generation would live up to their name. They started well, beating England 3-2 in the first group game, with Figo scoring an absolute worldie.

Portugal played brilliantly throughout the tournament, but they came up against World Cup champions France in the semis and lost to a golden goal.

That fateful return to Barcelona was like something out of a horror movie. On 21 October 2000, the best player in Europe stepped onto the Camp Nou turf for the first time as a Real player. The noise of the crowd was deafening, and the shock could be seen on all of the players' faces. Every time Figo went to take a corner, he was pelted with lighters, bottles, coins and anything the Barcelona fans had close. It was disgraceful.

Somehow, he got through the game, his head never dropping. He did look stunned, though, and he was probably wondering just how the 98,000 people hissing at him had forgotten everything he did for their club. Amazingly, that wasn't the worst of it.

The next time Real played at Barca, the noise was worse. People thought the fans might have simmered down since they'd had another year to deal with the transfer, but they hadn't. One of the most famous moments in the Real-Barca rivalry occurred when someone in the crowd threw a pig's head at Figo. Yes, a pig's head!

Figo won the league in his first year, which must have felt nice after the way he'd been treated by Barcelona. As the first Galácticos signed, he was surely delighted when the following year, the second arrived—Zinedine Zidane!

Together, they won the 2002 Champions League, with Zidane scoring one of the greatest goals the competition has ever seen. By now, Figo had also become Portugal's captain and was at the peak of his powers. When the 2002 World Cup rolled around, Portugal were expected to do big things.

They didn't, and getting dumped out by South Korea was one of Figo's lowest points.

As we covered in the Cristiano Ronaldo section, Portugal hosted the 2004 Euros only to lose to underdog Greece in the final. If the Korea loss was one of Figo's low points, then slipping up in the final of the Euros was surely his biggest disappointment.

After his successful time at Real, Figo joined Inter Milan in 2005. In the four seasons he spent in Italy, he won the league four times! He captained Portugal at the 2006 World Cup, helping the team to the semifinals. It was the first time they'd got that far since Eusébio's Portugal in 1966.

He retired from international football after the World Cup, handing down his number 7 jersey to one Cristiano Ronaldo. Not a bad replacement, really!

MARCO VAN BASTEN

Teams

AJAX
1981–1987
APPS – 132, GLS – 127

↓

AC MILAN
1987–1995
APPS – 147, GLS – 91

Trophy Cabinet

EUROS	X1
BALLON D'OR	X3
SERIE A CHAMPION	X3
EUROPEAN CHAMPION CLUBS' CUP	X2
DUTCH CHAMPION	X3

International Stats

CAPS	GOALS
58	24

BIOGRAPHY

BORN	OCT 31, 1964
NATIONALITY	DUTCH
STRONG FOOT	RIGHT
HEIGHT	1.88M
RETIRED	1995

A few of the players on this list suffered injuries throughout their careers, but none of them went through the agony Marco van Basten did. His injuries were so bad that he had to retire at 28, but he crammed more into his decade of playing than just about anyone. In that time, he won three Ballon d'Ors, three Eredivisie titles, four Serie A titles, two European Cups and the Euros with Holland!

As a pure number 9, there probably hasn't been anyone better. Marco van Basten was unplayable in his prime. He had pace, size, agility, an eye for goal, intelligence and the ability to score the spectacular as well as tap-ins. Most finishers who grew up in the '80s and '90s claim him as their inspiration.

Marcel "Marco" van Basten was born in Utrecht, Holland, on 31 October 1964. He grew up watching the fantastic Holland team of the '70s, and he especially loved Johan Cruyff. Little did he know that when he made his Ajax debut a few years later, he would be subbed on for the great man!

His youth career began at his hometown club, Utrecht, but Ajax snapped him up when he was 16. He played one season in their youth team before they couldn't hold him back any longer, and he made his debut at 17. As mentioned, he was subbed on for his hero, and a few minutes later, he scored his first senior goal!

His international debut came that year, too, playing alongside fellow teenagers Ruud Gullit, Frank Rijkaard and Ronald Koeman. All would go on to be Dutch legends.

Marco was trying to break into the Ajax team at a time when they had Wim Kieft as their number 9. Another Dutch legend, Wim, had been Europe's top scorer the previous year, so he wasn't going to give up his spot easily! As Wim's understudy*, Marco scored nine in his 20 games that season.

Amazingly, Ajax sold Wim Kieft the following summer, feeling that Marco was too good to hold back. He was just 18!

Marco immediately settled into the first team, finishing with the league's Golden Boot in his first season as the main man. He would do the same thing in his next three campaigns. In the 1985–86 season, he scored 37 goals in 26 league games, including a double hat trick in a game against Sparta Rotterdam. He also scored the winning goal in that year's Cup Winners' Cup final.

By 1987, Marco was the best young player on the planet, and the world's best team at the time, AC Milan, came calling. They snapped him up while also signing fellow Dutch hero Ruud Gullit. At a time when Italy (and most European countries) only allowed three foreign players, teams had to be very precise with who they signed. Milan also brought in Frank Rijkaard the following year, so they had Holland's three best players!

Marco van Basten left Ajax having scored 127 goals in 133 games.

A pretty cool thing happened around this time. Inter Milan, AC's biggest rivals, used their three foreigner slots to sign Germany's three best players—Jürgen Klinsmann, Lothar Matthäus and Andreas Brehme. With Germany and Holland also having a fierce rivalry, this made everything more interesting!

The summer after signing for AC Milan, Marco had his best moment in a Holland shirt. At Euro 88, Holland were drawn in a tough group against the Soviet Union, one of the best teams in the world at the time. They also had England and Ireland! In the opening game against the Soviets, Holland lost 1-0. It looked like they'd blown it.

Against England, Marco stepped up, banging in a hat trick in a 3-1 win. In the semis, they met West Germany, and the game was even more interesting because of the links between Inter Milan and AC Milan. Marco scored the winner in a 2-1 win to send Holland into the final, where they would again face the Soviets.

After Ruud Gullit gave Holland the lead in the 32nd minute, Marco van Basten saved the best for last. With 54 minutes gone, he was found on the edge of the box with a long diagonal pass. The ball seemed to take an age to drop, but van Basten watched it all the way. Just as it looked like he was running out of pitch, he caught it on the volley, whipping the ball past the keeper into the opposite top corner. It is still seen as the greatest goal ever scored at the Euros.

Holland won the tournament, which is amazingly the only major silverware they've ever won. Marco won his first Ballon d'Or at the end of the season.

The following year, Marco won the Ballon d'Or for the second year running. He scored 32 goals for Milan as they won the European Cup, with Marco and Gullit scoring two each in the final. They won it again the following year, beating Benfica 1–0.

The 1990 World Cup was a disaster, as Holland went in as favourites, only to crash out to the old enemy, West Germany, in the first knockout round. It was van Basten's only World Cup, and he failed to score a goal.

At his club, he was untouchable, which was proven when legendary coach Arrigo Sacchi was fired for falling out with him. Fabio Capello took over, and Milan became unstoppable, going unbeaten to win the league. The unbeaten run lasted well into the following season and didn't end until the 59th game.

In 1992, Marco became the first player to score four goals in a Champions League game (it had just changed from the European Cup), including one of his trademark bicycle kicks. He won the FIFA World Player of the Year and the Ballon d'Or for the third time. People were saying he would be the greatest ever if he kept going like he was. Sadly, that never happened.

The rest of Marco van Basten's career can be summed up as "horrible injury, failed recovery, horrible injury". He never really got more than a couple of games in before another horrific injury sidelined him again. In the end, he was forced to retire at 28. At his farewell appearance at the San Siro, Fabio Capello (and most of the crowd) cried uncontrollably.

The world has never seen a finisher like Marco van Basten before or since. He was truly one of a kind.

THIERRY HENRY

TEAMS

MONACO
1994-1999
APPS – 105, GLS – 20
↓
JUVENTUS
1999
APPS – 16, GLS – 3
↓
ARSENAL
1999-2007
APPS – 254, GLS – 174
↓
BARCELONA
2007-2010
APPS – 80, GLS – 35
↓
NEW YORK RED BULLS
2010-2014
APPS – 122, GLS – 51
↓
ARSENAL (LOAN)
2012
APPS – 4, GLS – 1

TROPHY CABINET

WORLD CUP	X1
EUROS	X1
CHAMPIONS LEAGUE	X1
PREMIER LEAGUE CHAMPION	X2
FA CUP	X3
LA LIGA CHAMPION	X2

INTERNATIONAL STATS

CAPS	GOALS
123	51

BIOGRAPHY

BORN	AUG 17, 1977
NATIONALITY	FRENCH
STRONG FOOT	RIGHT
HEIGHT	1.88M
RETIRED	DEC 16, 2014

The "Panenka penalty". The "Cruyff turn". The "Ronaldo celebration". These are all things that are part of football's dictionary and were named after the player who created them. The same can be said for the "Henry finish" when a player casually slots the ball into the bottom corner with the inside of their foot.

But Thierry Henry was so much more than a signature finish—he was the most devastating forward in Premier League history. Strangely, he started out as a winger, and his Premier League story didn't start too well, either. In fact, it took him seven games just to find the back of the net!

Once he did score, he didn't stop, and by the time he left for Barcelona and even more glory, he was talked about as one of the all-time greats.

Born in Les Ulis, Paris, on 17 August 1977, Thierry Henry grew up in a tough neighbourhood. It was tough, but it was also a great place for young footballers, as it had plenty of top facilities. At 7, he was already being spoken about, but young Thierry wasn't that fussed about football. It took a few years for him to fall in love with the sport he would one day dominate.

When Thierry was 13, Monaco, one of the biggest clubs in France, sent a scout to watch him play. He scored all six goals in a 6–0 win, and the scout asked him to sign right there and then. He didn't even have to attend a trial!

He joined the famous Clairefontaine academy, the place where most of France's greatest-ever players first learned their trade. After coming through the ranks, he joined Monaco's first team, which was managed by his future Arsenal manager, Arsène Wenger.

After a slowish start to his career, Henry really took off in 1996, winning the French Young Footballer of the Year. The following season, he helped Monaco to the league title. He was still being played as a winger, but Wenger knew that Henry's real future was up front.

When France held the World Cup in 1998, nobody—especially the French supporters—expected them to do anything. But everything seemed to click, with Henry out on the wing and Zinedine Zidane controlling things in the middle of the park. Still, when they met Brazil and Ronaldo in the final, it was thought that France's form would come to an end. Instead, they won 3–0, and Henry was a world champion at 21!

A year later, he was on his way to Juventus, but he found it hard in Italy, as the coaches didn't seem to understand how to use him properly. He was even played at wing back a few times! After only six months and three goals with Juventus, Henry teamed up with Arsène Wenger once more, this time at Arsenal.

It was at Arsenal where Henry would play the best football of his career. Despite his slow start, he was soon becoming the most feared forward in England. With his electric pace, strength, agility and coolness under pressure, he was the perfect partner for Dennis Bergkamp, who delighted in threading players through from his number 10 position.

Henry was now being played up front, but with his instinct to drop out wide, he often found himself between the lines. It made him an absolute nightmare for defenders to mark, as they didn't know whether to stick or twist. But despite his great personal stats in the beginning, Arsenal kept just missing out on the top prizes. That all changed in the 2001–02 season when they did the double, beating Manchester United in their own stadium to clinch the league.

Although he had struggled for silverware in his first couple of years with Arsenal, the medals continued to come for France, as he led the line and the team to victory at Euro 2000.

The 2002–03 season was immense for Henry on a personal level, as he finished the year with 32 goals and 23 assists, helping Arsenal to the FA Cup along the way. If that season was good, the following one was incredible. In fact, it was "invincible".

Arsenal went unbeaten in the 2003–04 season, creating the Invincibles tag that they will always be remembered by. Henry was in total beast mode as Arsenal became the only team in modern-day football to go unbeaten in England's top flight. He scored and assisted more than the previous year and won a string of individual awards.

Henry continued to be a legend for Arsenal for several more seasons, but the team was going through a transition, and only a single FA Cup followed. In the summer of 2007, he moved to Barcelona, feeling that it would be the only way for him to win the Champions League. He left Arsenal as their all-time leading goalscorer, and a statue of him was erected outside the Emirates Stadium.

In the 2008–09 season, Henry formed a devastating partnership with Lionel Messi and Samuel Eto'o, and they scored 100 goals between them in one year. Barca won the league, the Spanish Cup and the Champions League. The last of these meant that Henry had won everything there was to win in football.

Barca followed this up with the next three trophies available to them, giving them the unimaginable sextuple. It was a ridiculous achievement for everyone involved, and that team will always go down in history as one of the best ever. That Barca side was incredible.

Henry moved to the New York Red Bulls in 2010, and a couple of years later, he made an emotional return to Arsenal on loan, scoring on his second debut. He won a couple of Eastern Conferences in his four and a half years in New York before retiring in 2014.

At his peak, Thierry Henry was insane. He is often called the best player to have played in England, and if you ever saw him in his prime, that's pretty hard to argue!

ROMÁRIO
DE SOUZA FARIA

Teams

Team	Years	Apps	Gls
VASCO DA GAMA	1985–1988	141	80
PSV EINDHOVEN	1988–1993	110	98
BARCELONA	1993–1995	46	34
FLAMENGO	1995–1996	59	60
VALENCIA	1996–1997	11	5
FLAMENGO	1997–1999	87	55
VASCO DA GAMA	2000–2002	73	79
FLUMINENSE	2002–2004	73	45
VASCO DA GAMA	2005–2006	50	35
MIAMI FC	2006	25	19
VASCO DA GAMA	2007	15	13

Trophy Cabinet

WORLD CUP	X1
COPA AMÉRICA	X2
LA LIGA CHAMPION	X1
DUTCH CHAMPION	X3
DUTCH CUP	X3
BRAZILIAN CHAMPION	X1

International Stats

CAPS	GOALS
70	55

BIOGRAPHY

BORN	JAN 29, 1966
NATIONALITY	BRAZILIAN
STRONG FOOT	RIGHT
HEIGHT	1.67M
RETIRED	2009

Another player who defenders often claimed was their toughest opponent, Romário, was a goal-scoring machine. Small, compact, yet lightning quick and sharp, he was devastating in and around the box. Famed for his classic toe-poke finish, he shredded defenders, who sometimes didn't even know he had skinned them until the ball was in the net.

Born and raised in a poverty-stricken neighbourhood in Rio de Janeiro on 29 January 1966, Romário de Souza Faria grew up with only one dream—to become a professional footballer. He trained hard, often coming up against boys twice his size. He quickly learned to use his small frame to his advantage, so he practised getting the ball out of tight spaces and finishing quickly. This would become his trademark as he developed.

Vasco da Gama spotted him playing as a teenager, and he quickly worked his way up through the youth ranks. After a few years in the first team, where he scored 80 goals in 141 games, he finally earned his transfer to Europe, where he knew the world's best players competed. He joined PSV Eindhoven in 1988, just as he was breaking into the Brazil national side.

At PSV, he became a goal-scoring beast, netting at a ratio of a goal a game. Romário was earning a reputation as a laid-back player who had complete belief in his ability. Some would have called it arrogance, but he was just confident. He was known to sit next to a worried teammate or coach in the dressing room and tell them to relax and that he would score a few and the team would win!

He etched his name forever in Brazilian hearts at the 1989 Copa América when he scored the only goal in a 1–0 win against Uruguay in the final. Brazil had gone a long, long time without a trophy, and that win was massive for them. That same year, he won his first title with PSV, finishing as the league's top scorer. He won the league again in 1991 and 1992 before Barcelona came calling.

In the leadup to the 1990 World Cup, Romário was one of the most hyped strikers in the world. Still young, he was expected to lead Brazil's attack and the team to glory. They hadn't won the World Cup since Pelé's last in 1970, and two decades is a long time for a nation like Brazil to go without winning the big one.

Sadly, Romário suffered a terrible knee injury right before the tournament, but he was so good that he was still included in the squad. He only managed 65 minutes of one group game as Brazil crashed out in the second round following a 1–0 loss to arch-enemies Argentina.

Romário's move to Barcelona was big news, as manager Johan Cruyff was building what he called the Dream Team. They already had Hristo Stoichkov and Michael Laudrup, two forwards who could have easily made this list. On top of that, they had superstars such as Ronald Koeman and José Mari Bakero. With

Romário having scored 165 goals in 167 games for PSV, he was always going to fit in!

In his first season in Spain, Romário won the Pichichi with 30 goals in 33 games, helping Barca win the league. That same year, they reached the Champions League final in what was seen as a beauty and the beast clash with Fabio Capello's AC Milan. Cruyff had claimed in the buildup that AC Milan were a boring, defensive team while his Barca boys played silky football.

Cruyff's trash-talk backfired, and Milan smashed Barca 4–0.

In the buildup to the 1994 World Cup, Romário fell out with the national team's manager. He was kicked out of the squad for seven qualifying games, in which Brazil lost one of them to Bolivia. It was the first time the team had ever lost a qualifying game, and the public demanded that Romário be recalled.

The manager gave in to the pressure and brought Romário back into the team for the final qualifying game. Brazil needed to beat Uruguay to top the group, and Romário scored both goals in a 2–0 win.

At the World Cup itself, he was on fire. He scored in all three group games, including a trademark toe-poke goal against Sweden. He then scored one of the goals of the tournament against Holland in the quarterfinals and then headed home the winner against Sweden in the semis. The final was one of the worst of all time—a dull 0–0 draw with Italy—but Romário scored his penalty in the shootout as Brazil lifted the World Cup for the first time in 24 years.

One surprising fact is that Romário played for Barcelona for less than two years. This is strange because it is often the club we most associate him with. We remember him in the Barcelona colours simply because he was the best finisher in the world during that period.

He moved to Flamengo in Brazil after falling out with Cruyff, but his legacy with Barca was cemented. One of his best moments came against Real Madrid when he scored a wonderful hat trick in a 5-0 win. Letting him go so soon is still seen as one of Barcelona's worst mistakes.

In the leadup to the 1998 World Cup, Romário formed a powerful partnership with Ronaldo, which was sadly broken up right before the tournament when Romário picked up an injury. He was in tears as he told reporters he wouldn't be fit enough to make the squad.

He spent five and a half years with Flamengo before becoming a bit of a journeyman*. He played for clubs in Brazil, Qatar, the USA and even Australia before finally retiring in 2008.

A year before he retired, Romário scored the 1000th goal of his career while playing for the club where it all started for him, Vasco da Gama. When the ball hit the net, the game was stopped for 20 minutes while everyone partied on the pitch! His 1,000 goals were proof—if anyone really needed it—that he was one of the best finishers of all time.

RIVALDO
VÍTOR BORBA FERREIRA

TEAMS

SANTA CRUZ 1990–1992 — APPS – 9, GLS – 1

CORINTHIANS (LOAN) 1993–1994 — APPS – 8, GLS – 2

PALMEIRAS 1994–1996 — APPS – 30, GLS – 14

DEPORTIVO LA CORUÑA 1996–1997 — APPS – 41, GLS – 21

BARCELONA 1997–2002 — APPS – 157, GLS – 86

AC MILAN 2002–2003 — APPS – 22, GLS – 5

CRUZEIRO 2004 — APPS – 11, GLS – 2

OLYMPIACOS 2004–2007 — APPS – 70, GLS – 36

AEK ATHENS 2007–2008 — APPS – 35, GLS – 12

BUNYODKOR 2008–2011 — APPS – 53, GLS – 33

SÃO PAULO (LOAN) 2011 — APPS – 30, GLS – 5

KABUSCORP 2012 — APPS – 21, GLS – 11

TROPHY CABINET

WORLD CUP	X1
COPA AMÉRICA	X1
BALLON D'OR	X1
CHAMPIONS LEAGUE	X1
LA LIGA CHAMPION	X2
SERIE A CHAMPION	X1

INTERNATIONAL STATS

CAPS	GOALS
74	35

BIOGRAPHY

BORN	APRIL 19, 1972
NATIONALITY	BRAZILIAN
STRONG FOOT	LEFT
HEIGHT	1.86M
RETIRED	AUG 2015

We've covered Ronaldo (R9) and Ronaldinho, and now we have the third part of what became known as "the three Rs". Brazil's attack at the 2002 World Cup was phenomenal, and Rivaldo was the player who made the three Rs gel. He is probably the least known of the trio, but he was unreal. He is also one of the nine players to have won the Ballon d'Or, the World Cup and the Champions League.

A lot of the players on this list grew up poor, but probably none of them went through the sort of poverty Rivaldo had to suffer. In fact, he was malnourished* as a kid, and he still shows the scars today. He lost several teeth, and his legs are slightly warped due to being bow-legged*. To come through all of that and reach the very top of the football world takes determination beyond belief.

Born in Recife, Brazil, Rivaldo grew up in the favelas*. At times, his hunger was so bad that he would be bedridden. Whenever his strength would allow it, he would play football. Despite his weakness, he was tall and gangly, and his left foot was ridiculous. Unfortunately, most teams were unsure about signing him as a kid, as they felt he was just too unwell.

In the end, a small Brazilian team who weren't even in Serie C (Brazilian third division) decided to take a shot on him. That team was Paulistano Futebol Clube, and they offered him a youth contract when he was 16.

Much like Luís Figo, Rivaldo had to gradually work his way up. And to make matters worse, his father died in a car crash just weeks before he signed for Paulistano. Rivaldo knew that he had to give it everything. If he didn't, he would spend the rest of his life in poverty.

Two years after signing for Paulistano, he joined Santa Cruz, who were a slightly bigger club. He spent a year there, improving with each game before he was bought by Mogi Mirim, a team in the Brazilian second division. He did another year of improving before one of the big boys came in, and he signed for Corinthians on loan.

Despite only playing eight times for Corinthians, their fans were still furious when he signed with their bitter rivals Palmeiras in 1993. The move was great for Rivaldo, though, and he finally found a team that knew how to use him. In his first season, he won the league, which was made even sweeter when he earned his first Brazil cap, scoring in a friendly against Mexico.

Rivaldo's body shape and running style made it hard for coaches to figure out just what position suited him best. Even now, years after his retirement, fans still argue over his best position. As a number 10, he was brilliant, and he could create a goal just as easily as score one. He could play as the main striker, and even off the wing where he could cut in on his left and score. Inside or outside the box, he was dangerous.

After a couple of years with Palmeiras, he moved to Spain, signing for Deportivo de La Coruña, who were a top team at the time. He only spent one year there, scoring 21 goals in 41 matches before Barcelona snapped him up. He was signed as a replacement for Ronaldo (R9), who had joined Inter Milan.

At first, the Barca fans didn't take to Rivaldo. Ronaldo was a dynamic goal machine, whereas Rivaldo was more elegant and drifted around the pitch. When the team won the double at the end of Rivaldo's first season, the fans quickly changed their minds about him!

When Romário's injury kept him out of the 1998 World Cup, Rivaldo was brought into the starting lineup to play alongside Ronaldo. They instantly clicked, and their partnership brought the team all the way to the final. As we know, Ronaldo suffered a seizure, and France won 3-0.

Rivaldo's club form continued to improve, and after retaining the league in 1999, he was awarded the FIFA Player of the Year award and the Ballon d'Or. That same year, he helped Brazil win the Copa América, finishing as the tournament's top scorer, netting twice in a 3-0 win over Uruguay in the final.

Despite him continuing to boss it at Barca, the team was now struggling. By the 2000-01 season, they were mid-table. After a strong end to the season, they clawed their way up to fifth with one game left to play. That game was against Valencia, who were Champions League finalists and one of the best teams in Europe. They were also the team in fourth. If Barca wanted Champions League football the following season, they needed to win.

Rivaldo scored what is widely seen as the greatest hat trick of all time to help Barca to a 3–2 win. His first goal was a whipped free kick that left the stadium breathless. His second saw him shimmy and feint, leaving the defence chasing shadows before slamming the ball into the bottom corner from 25 yards. He saved the best for last, though.

With 89 minutes gone and the score 2–2, Rivaldo took a long ball on his chest 18 yards from goal. As it looped into the air, he angled his body and scored a spectacular bicycle kick to win the match. It was insane, and he had forever written himself into Barcelona legend.

Amazingly, he was sold a year later, moving to AC Milan. In his only season with Milan, he won the Champions League, but his game time wasn't what he wanted, and he moved on.

That same year, the three Rs ran riot at the 2002 World Cup. Rivaldo scored five in the opening five games, while Ronaldo scored four. Ronaldinho scored that amazing free kick against England after Rivaldo had scored the equaliser, and he then went on to play a part in both of Ronaldo's goals in the final. It was the crowning moment of Rivaldo's amazing career.

After a successful spell in Greece with Olympiacos, where he scored the goal that won the team the league in his second season, he moved around a lot. Rivaldo played for many different clubs, including two more spells at Mogi Mirim, one of his earliest clubs. He retired in 2014, but played one more game in 2015, lining up next to his son, Rivaldinho, who was playing for Mogi Mirim at the time.

In that game, both father and son scored, creating the perfect moment for Rivaldo to finally hang up his boots!

LUIS SUÁREZ

Teams

Team	Years	Apps	Gls
NACIONAL	2005–2006	27	10
GRONINGEN	2006–2007	29	10
AJAX	2007–2011	110	81
LIVERPOOL	2011–2014	110	69
BARCELONA	2014–2020	191	147
ATLÉTICO MADRID	2020–2022	67	32
NACIONAL	2022	14	8
GRÊMIO	2023–2024	45	24
INTER MIAMI	2024–	18	12

Trophy Cabinet

COPA AMÉRICA	x1
CHAMPIONS LEAGUE	x1
LA LIGA CHAMPION	x5
SPANISH CUP	x4
ENGLISH LEAGUE CUP	x1
DUTCH CHAMPION	x1

International Stats

CAPS	GOALS
142	69

BIOGRAPHY

BORN	JAN 24, 1987
NATIONALITY	URUGUAYAN
STRONG FOOT	RIGHT
HEIGHT	1.82M
RETIRED	STILL PLAYING

Although he is still playing at the time of this book being written, Luis Suárez has already cemented his reputation as one of the best strikers of all time. He has never done things the easy way, and some of his disciplinary issues have often overshadowed his talent on the pitch. From biting opponents to his nasty fallout with Patrice Evra, Luis Suárez has always been the type of player who is hated by opposing fans but adored by his own.

Born on 24 January 1987 in Salto, Uruguay, Luis was the fourth of seven kids, all of them boys! When he was seven, the family moved to Montevideo, and Luis found himself playing a lot of street football. All of his brothers were football crazy, just like him, so he always had someone to have a kickabout with!

When he was 14, he was spotted by scouts for the top Uruguayan club, Nacional, and he signed for their youth team.

The aggression and anger that would follow him through his career was always there, and at 16, Luis was sent off in a youth team game after headbutting the referee. Still, Nacional believed in his talents, and they encouraged him to keep training and improving. Soon, he was called up to the first team.

Luis Suárez made his senior debut at 17, coming off the

bench in a Copa Libertadores match against Atlético Junior. A few months later, he scored his first senior goal. It would be one of many to come!

By the following year, Luis was already a regular, and he scored 10 goals in 27 matches as Nacional won the league. Luis was still raw, but Dutch side Groningen saw how good he was, and they signed him that summer. Luis had always dreamed of playing in Europe, but he never expected it to happen so soon. He had just turned 19.

His dream soon became a nightmare, and he suffered from homesickness. To help fit in, he spent hours each day learning Dutch, and after a tough first season, he finally started to settle into his new surroundings. As soon as he did, he took off.

After impressing with Groningen, Dutch giants Ajax came in for him. They offered €3.5 million, which Groningen rejected. Luis knew he couldn't miss the chance to play for such a massive club, and he took Groningen to court to try and force the move. The judge ruled against him, but later that day, Ajax doubled their bid, and it was accepted!

His first game for Uruguay was bittersweet. They beat Columbia 3–1, but Luis was sent off near the end of the game.

Back at Ajax, he quickly formed a great partnership with Klaas-Jan Huntelaar. His manager, Marco van Basten, knew that Suárez could be one of the greats, but he worried about his discipline. Red and yellow cards seemed to be a part of the deal when you had

Luis Suárez in the team!

In his first season, Luis scored 17 goals, and followed this up with 22 the next year. The season after that, he was named captain. That season—2009-10—he was unreal. In one game against WHC Wezep, he scored a double hat trick. He also netted four in two other games, and a hat trick in another. He ended the year with 49 goals in all competitions.

One of his most controversial moments came at the 2010 World Cup. Uruguay were having a great tournament, and when they got Ghana in the quarterfinals, it was seen as a wonderful chance to get further than they had done in decades. With the game tied at 1-1 in extra time, it looked like it would go to penalties, until Ghana got one last chance right at the end.

As the ball got flicked toward the Uruguay net, Suárez dived to the top corner and blocked the ball with his hand, stopping a certain winning goal. A penalty was given, and Suárez was instantly sent off. As he watched from the sidelines, Asamoah Gyan missed the spot kick, and Uruguay went on to win the penalty shootout.

Suárez was a villain once more, yet he was also a hero to his team and their fans. He was suspended for the semifinal against Holland as Uruguay crashed out following a 3-2 loss.

Suárez moved to Liverpool soon after scoring his 100th goal for Ajax. During his time at Anfield, he quickly became one of the most feared strikers in

Europe. When he arrived, Liverpool were struggling in mid-table. It took Suárez a few years to get the team up to his level, but they were soon challenging for the league. A comical Steven Gerrard slip against Chelsea handed the league to Manchester City, but Suárez had been immense for a couple of seasons.

After three years at Liverpool and only a League Cup winner's medal to show for it, Luis forced a move to Barcelona. He instantly formed one of the most devastating trios in history with Lionel Messi and Neymar. In his first season, Barcelona did the treble, including the Champions League. His decision to move had been proven correct beyond doubt.

That 2014–15 season saw Suárez, Neymar and Messi score 122 goals between them. If you think you read that wrong, you didn't. They really scored 122 goals in one season!

Barcelona retained the league the following year, with Suárez scoring even more. He was also assisting a massive amount for his teammates, something which he had always done in the past. He won the European Golden Shoe for the second time in his career.

The 2017–18 season saw Barca doing the double while going on a record-breaking 43-game unbeaten run. By the time he left the Catalan club, his trophy cabinet was bursting! He moved to Atlético Madrid, where he won the league in his first season while also being named as Atlético's player of the year.

After two seasons with Atlético, he re-signed with Nacional, and in the first season of his second spell there, he won the league! He also scored two hat tricks that season, finishing with 17 goals and 11 assists. He was named Player of the Year.

Luis Suárez has since signed for Inter Miami, where he hooked up with former Barca teammates Lionel Messi, Sergio Busquets and Jordi Alba. He is 37 at the time of this book being written, so he probably has another few seasons left in him!

RAÚL
GONZÁLEZ BLANCO

Teams

REAL MADRID
1994–2010
APPS – 550, GLS – 228

↓

SCHALKE 04
2010–2012
APPS – 66, GLS – 28

↓

AL SADD
2012–2014
APPS – 39, GLS – 11

↓

NEW YORK COSMOS
2014–2015
APPS – 28, GLS – 8

Trophy Cabinet

CHAMPIONS LEAGUE	X3
LA LIGA CHAMPION	X6
SPANISH SUPER CUP	X4
UEFA SUPERCUP	X1
INTERCONTINENTAL CUP	X2
GERMAN CUP	X1

International Stats

CAPS	GOALS
102	44

BIOGRAPHY

BORN	JUNE 27, 1977
NATIONALITY	SPANISH
STRONG FOOT	RIGHT
HEIGHT	1.8M
RETIRED	2014

Before the Galácticos, there was just Raúl. For what seemed like an age, he was Real Madrid's best player and biggest star. He was and is "Mr Madrid". He has had more appearances for the club than any other player in history, and he is their third-highest scorer.

As a number 9, he was a top-class finisher. His left foot was capable of stroking the ball home or slamming it from 25 yards if needed. He was calm under pressure, and with the ability to drop deep and create just as easily as score, Raúl was one of the most prolific* forwards in history.

Raúl González Blanco was born in Madrid on 27 June 1977, and he grew up obsessed with football. It was all he wanted to do. He played every minute he could, and it wasn't long before he was snapped up by Atlético Madrid. Yep, it was actually Real's fierce rivals who had him first!

Raúl spent his childhood and early teens training in Atlético's youth teams. Then, in the early 1990s, Atlético owner Jesús Gil decided that the youth system was costing too much money, so he scrapped it! All of the kids on Atlético's books were released. At 16, Raúl signed for Real.

His rise through the youth ranks at Real was rapid. After one season, he was promoted to the C team. He played nine games with them before moving up to the B team. It took only one game at that level before he was called up to the senior team. Unlike their neighbours, Atlético, Real Madrid knew they had a top player on their books.

Raúl made his debut at just 17 years and 124 days old, coming on as a substitute away to Real Zaragoza. It made him Real's youngest-ever player, and he instantly made an impact by setting up a goal. In his very next game, he made his home debut in one of Real's biggest matches every year—they faced Atlético Madrid!

Raúl scored against the team that had let him go, instantly forming a bond with the Real fans in the process. From that moment on, he was Real's darling.

Raúl quickly became a regular, and in his first season with Madrid, they won the league!

His first cap for Spain came soon after, and on 9 October 1996, he played the full match against the Czech Republic in a World Cup qualifier. He scored his first international goal a couple of games later.

Real won the title again in 1997, with Raúl scoring 21 goals. He was still just 20, yet he was the main man at the biggest club in the world. That year also saw the second rise of Real Madrid as the most dominant force in Europe. They won the Champions League three times in the next four years, with Raúl scoring in two of the finals.

The first rise was that amazing five in a row we

covered in the Puskás and Di Stéfano sections. Real did it again in recent times, with Cristiano Ronaldo leading the charge!

At just 21, Raúl led the line for Spain at the 1998 World Cup. He scored in their opening match, but Spain were awful and went out in the group stage. Up until they won the Euros in 2008 and went on to dominate world football for six or seven years, Spain were the biggest underachievers in the game.

His form continued to reach crazy levels, and in a Euro qualifying game against Austria in 1999, Raúl scored four as Spain won 9–0. He scored another hat trick four days later as they thumped San Marino 6–0.

After winning the Champions League in 1998, Madrid were in the final again in 2000. They beat fellow Spaniards Valencia 3–0, with Raúl rounding off the scoring with a typical cool finish. He went into Euro 2000 as one of the deadliest strikers in world football, but it ended in heartbreak as Spain lost on penalties to France in the quarterfinals. Raúl missed a penalty in injury time that would have taken the game into extra time.

The 2002 Champions League final will be forever known as Zidane's final due to his stunning left-footed volley to win the game, but people often forget that it was Raúl who opened the scoring. Real won 2–1 against Leverkusen, and Raúl had his third Champions League medal.

The 2002 World Cup was another disappointment, as Spain were humbled by South Korea, who knocked them out in the quarters. Raúl had been banging the goals in throughout the tournament, but he picked up an injury in the previous round and missed the Korea game.

He was given the Madrid captaincy in 2003, a role he proudly held onto for another seven years. Two years later, he became the first player in history to score 50 Champions League goals, and he was also the first player to reach 100 Champions League games. He was also the first to score in two separate finals.

Raúl won his 100th cap for Spain on 15 August 2006 in a game against Iceland and then played his last international match a few months later. On 11 November 2008, he scored his 300th Madrid goal, then followed it up a few weeks later by surpassing Alfredo Di Stéfano's 307 Real goals!

Amazingly, that same year, Raúl and fellow Real legend Iker Casillas were offered "contracts for life". It basically meant that as long as they were fit enough to play, they could have a contract!

His final game for Madrid was like something out of a Hollywood movie. Halfway through the second period, Raúl picked up an injury. As he hobbled around, he told the bench that he needed to come off. They had Karim Benzema ready when Cristiano Ronaldo broke clear. Raúl somehow shuffled his way into the box and slotted Ronaldo's ball home. He was then subbed off.

This happened in a match against Real Zaragoza, at their home ground, where he had made his Real debut. His injury kept him out for the rest of the season, and he never played for them again. His last touch in a Real shirt was a goal!

Two years in Germany followed, where he won the DFB-Pokal (German Cup) with Schalke 04. Spells in Qatar and America were short and sweet before Raúl moved into management, taking over Real's C and then B team. It's almost a certainty that he will manage the first team soon. He is Mr Madrid, after all!

ROBERTO BAGGIO

Teams

VICENZA
1982-1985
APPS - 36, GLS - 13

FIORENTINA
1985-1990
APPS - 94, GLS - 39

JUVENTUS
1990-1995
APPS - 141, GLS - 78

AC MILAN
1995-1997
APPS - 51, GLS - 12

BOLOGNA
1997-1998
APPS - 30, GLS - 22

INTER MILAN
1998-2000
APPS - 41, GLS - 9

BRESCIA
2000-2004
APPS - 95, GLS - 45

Trophy Cabinet

BALLON D'OR	X1
SERIE A CHAMPION	X2
UEFA CUP	X1
ITALIAN CUP	X1

International Stats

CAPS	GOALS
56	27

BIOGRAPHY

BORN	FEB 18, 1967
NATIONALITY	ITALIAN
STRONG FOOT	RIGHT
HEIGHT	1.74M
RETIRED	2004

The man known as "the Divine Ponytail" was something of a superhero. To come back (several times) from the horrific injuries he suffered takes unbelievable strength and courage. He played for a few clubs, and just about every one of them remembers him as a god.

More like a Brazilian or an Argentinian in how he played, Baggio was often left out of Italy squads despite the outrage of the fans. In the 1980s and '90s (and all through history, really), Italy have been a rigid team with no place for flair players. If Baggio had been born in South America or somewhere like Holland, he would have been his country's main man for decades.

Born in Caldogno, Veneto, on 18 February 1967, Roberto was the sixth of eight kids. His family struggled financially, and his father was extremely strict. Roberto's younger brother Eddie was also a good footballer who went on to play 86 games in Serie B.

Roberto was first spotted when he was 9, and his silky skills and flair made him stand out. He could play as a number 9, but as he grew up, he often preferred to drop a little deeper. This gave him more space to run at defenders, which he was one of the best in the world at. His finishing was exceptional, too.

He signed for his hometown club, Caldogno, and when

he was 11, he scored 45 goals and assisted 20 in just 26 matches! He was snapped up by Vicenza, who played in Serie C at the time.

Roberto had only just turned 16 when he made his senior debut and scored his first goal soon after. By the 1984–85 season, and at just 17, he was a regular, scoring 12 goals in 29 appearances. Vicenza won promotion to Serie B in his first full season, but they knew they couldn't hold onto their prize asset for much longer.

Fiorentina came in for him, and a verbal agreement was made as the season came to an end. Then tragedy struck. In one of the final games, Baggio shattered both ACLs* and the meniscus* in his right knee. The injury was so bad that all of his doctors told him his career was over. He was only 18.

Devastated but not defeated, he swore he would get fit again. To Fiorentina's credit, they went through with the deal regardless, even though there was a massive chance Roberto would never play again. They also paid for his surgeries.

He missed a season and a half recovering and didn't make his Fiorentina debut for nearly two years. When he did, he busted his knee again a few games into his return, this time needing 220 stitches to rebuild it. Somehow, he started and finished his treatment once more.

His first Fiorentina goal came on 10 May 1987 when he scored a stunning free kick to earn his team a draw against Maradona's Napoli. The result saved Fiorentina from relegation.

Roberto made his international debut in a 1988 friendly win over Holland. He was 21, but he would have surely broken into the team earlier if it weren't for his injuries.

The 1988–89 season was Baggio's breakthrough, as he helped Fiorentina shoot up the table. After just avoiding relegation by the skin of their teeth the previous year, Baggio helped to a 7th place finish and European football qualification!

He was still a surprise call-up for the Italian squad for World Cup 90, but only because of his style of play. In the end, he started all but one game as Italy reached the semifinals on home soil. The only game he didn't start was the last game against Argentina, as Italy lost on penalties, narrowly missing out on a place in the final.

Baggio scored the goal of the tournament, and one of the greatest goals of all time, as Italy beat Czechoslovakia. He drifted past several players before cutting inside and wrong-footing the keeper. He was now a global star!

After five years at Fiorentina, where he became a true legend, Baggio finally moved to one of the big teams. Juventus paid a then-world-record fee of £8 million (the record in England hadn't even gone past £3 million at the time), and he was given his favourite number 10 shirt.

His time at Juve wasn't great at first, as the fans struggled to take to him. As for the Fiorentina fans, they rioted in Florence, with 50 of them getting arrested. They couldn't believe the club had let their best player leave!

It was tough at Juve, as they were trying to catch that phenomenal AC Milan team of van Basten, Gullit and the rest. Still, they finished second in Baggio's second season and continued to close the gap.

Baggio was named captain for the 1992–93 season, and he led Juve to victory in the UEFA Cup. He scored two and assisted one over the two-legged final, and he ended the season with the FIFA World Player of the Year award and the Ballon d'Or. It meant he went into the 1994 World Cup as the best player around.

He was superb in that World Cup, scoring five goals and often carrying the team on his own as they reached the final. Sadly, his ballooned penalty in the shootout loss to Brazil became a meme, even before there were memes! Baggio has since claimed that he still has nightmares about the miss.

Juve won the league in 1995, but Baggio was already starting to be forced out. His time with Italy was becoming rough as well, as his managers refused to change their rigid systems to suit his class. Still, when Juve sold him to AC Milan, their fans rioted. This was becoming a recurring theme!

In his first season with Milan, they took the league back off Juve, which must have been nice for him. But his time at Milan was patchy, and as the 1998 World Cup approached, he left for Bologna to get more first team football.

Baggio cut off his ponytail and declared that it was a new beginning. His single season at Bologna was his personal best, as he scored 22 Serie A goals and provided nine assists. His gamble to leave Milan for a smaller club and first team football worked, and the national team had no choice but to recall him.

A move to Inter Milan followed, but it wasn't the best of times. At 33, and with people thinking he was past it, Baggio joined Brescia, who had just been promoted. He was named as captain and given his number 10, and then went on to lead them to a seventh-place finish!

He spent four years with Brescia before retiring, keeping them in Serie A throughout. In his last game, 80,000 packed into the San Siro to see him off, with most of them knowing they'd just seen the final moments of the most creative player ever to pull on an Italian shirt.

GEORGE BEST

Teams

Team	Years	Apps	Gls
MANCHESTER UNITED	1963–1974	361	137
STOCKPORT COUNTY	1975	3	2
CORK CELTIC	1975–1976	3	0
LOS ANGELES AZTECS	1976	23	15
FULHAM	1976–1977	42	8
LOS ANGELES AZTECS	1977–1978	32	12
FORT LAUDERDALE STRIKERS	1978–1979	28	6
HIBERNIAN	1979–1980	17	3
SAN JOSE EARTHQUAKES	1980–1981	56	21
AFC BOURNEMOUTH	1982–1983	5	0

Trophy Cabinet

- BALLON D'OR — X1
- ENGLISH CHAMPION — X2
- EUROPEAN CHAMPION CLUBS' CUP — X1
- FA CUP — X1
- ENGLISH SUPER CUP — X2

International Stats

CAPS	GOALS
37	9

BIOGRAPHY

BORN	MAY 22, 1946
NATIONALITY	NORTHERN IRISH
STRONG FOOT	RIGHT
HEIGHT	1.75M
RETIRED	1984

Much like Marco van Basten, George Best retired far too young. But unlike van Basten, who didn't have a choice, George Best kind of threw his career away. Still, in the ten years while he was playing, there was nobody like him.

At a time in England when players were expected to be clean-cut and boring, George Best was a rock star. With his pulled-down socks, untucked jersey, shaggy hair and stubble, George was a new breed. The older generation thought he was trouble, but the newer fans saw him as a hero.

George Best was born on 22 May 1946 in Cregagh, Belfast, at a time when Northern Ireland was a rough place to live. He was the oldest of five children, with four younger sisters who looked up to him. He was an exceptional player early on, although he was skinny, so he often had to deal with heavy tackles.

George was an extremely intelligent kid, but he was restless, and he would often skip school simply to find trouble. The only time he found peace, even as an adult, was on the football pitch.

While playing for his local club, George Best was spotted by a Manchester United scout. United were trying to rebuild their team after the Munich Air Disaster a few years before when the plane taking the team back to Manchester crashed while attempting to take off. Of the 44 people on board, 23 died. United's squad was destroyed, but legendary manager Sir Matt Busby, who survived, swore he would build the club back up again in honour of those who died.

The United scout who travelled to Northern Ireland in search of the next big thing is said to have watched George once before, instantly sending a telegram to Matt Busby saying, "I think I've found your genius."

George Best was one of the best dribblers in history, his casual style causing defenders to lose their cool and lunge in. He would skip by them in a flash, using his electric turn-of-pace to leave them in the dust. His finishing was unreal, and he loved nothing more than chipping the keeper or rounding him before tapping it into the net. He was one of the first true entertainers who believed that football was for the fans, so they should see magic on the pitch every week.

United signed George at 15, but two days after he arrived in Manchester, he returned to Belfast due to homesickness. His family convinced him to go back to Manchester and give it another go, as opportunities like that may not come around again. George agreed, and he soon got settled.

He spent less than two years in the youth setup before moving into the first team, making his debut on 14 September 1963 in a 1–0 win over West Bromwich Albion. He was just 17, and the fans who saw the skinny, scruffy kid waltz onto the pitch weren't overly excited. After a few touches and dribbles—the type they had only seen Brazilians do on TV—the fans were hooked. George Best was already their new darling.

When Best scored on his second appearance, Matt Busby knew he couldn't keep him out of the team much longer. He finished the season with six goals in 28 appearances, and United finished second in the league, a point behind Liverpool. It was a massive achievement, seeing as the Munich Air Disaster had happened just five years before.

In George's second season, United won the league, beating fierce rivals Leeds to the title on goal difference.

One of George's best moments came in the 1965–66 season when he was only 19. United had been drawn against Eusébio's Benfica in the quarterfinals of the European Cup. It was expected that the Portuguese legend would run riot, but it was United's superstar who ran the show. Best scored twice as United smashed Benfica 8–3 on aggregate, catapulting himself into fame no British player had experienced before.

George Best was one of the first players to do TV ads and endorsements*. Although many old pros disliked this, he inspired a whole generation of younger players who wanted to entertain on the pitch.

United won the league again in 1967, giving Sir Matt Busby another shot at the European Cup. No English team had ever won it, and he wanted United to be the first. As mentioned earlier in the book, only the league winners qualified, so the chance to win didn't come along as often as it does today.

The 1967–68 season was the ultimate one for both George and United. After beating European kings Real Madrid in the quarterfinals thanks to a world-class performance from Best, United came up against the other European giants of the era, Benfica.

Benfica knew what to expect this time, and they man-marked Best, fouling him relentlessly. Still, he managed to run the show, and when the game finished 1–1 and went to extra time, George stepped it up a level. His goal—beating a defender before dummying the keeper and slotting it home—gave United a 2–1 lead. Benfica collapsed, and the game ended 4–1.

George Best was a European champion and a two-time league winner at just 22. To top it off, he won the Ballon d'Or that summer, too!

Sadly, that success so young was the peak of his career. In the seasons that followed, Best continued to perform on the pitch, but he missed endless training sessions due to partying, drinking and living the high life. He once missed a whole week of training as he was cooped up in a hotel with Miss Great Britain!

Sir Matt Busby left United soon after the European Cup win, and with nobody to keep him in check, George went off the rails. Somehow, he finished six seasons on the spin as United's top scorer, but the team around him was getting worse each year.

Despite this, he still managed to score a double hat trick against Northampton in the FA Cup as United won 8–3. His sixth goal, where he feinted and dummied the poor keeper several times, leaving him sitting in the mud, is still one of the FA Cup's most iconic moments.

Even in the 1971–72 season, and with most of his coaches fining or suspending him every other week, George managed a couple of hat tricks in the league games against Southampton and West Ham while also scoring that year's goal of the season—a classic mazy run and finish against Sheffield United. It was his last season finishing as top scorer, and a couple of years later, with George out of the team, United were amazingly relegated.

George Best retired at 27. He spent a decade changing his mind, joining a team somewhere in Europe or America, and then retiring again. He usually got bored after a few weeks, or his manager got sick of his partying and sacked him. This was pretty much what his international career had been like, even when he was young. George only played for Northern Ireland 37 times, scoring just nine goals.

In his 10 years at the top, George Best was exactly what his name says—the Best!

DIEGO MARADONA

Teams

ARGENTINOS JUNIORS
1976-1981
APPS - 166, GLS - 116
↓
BOCA JUNIORS
1981-1982
APPS - 40, GLS - 28
↓
BARCELONA
1982-1984
APPS - 36, GLS - 22
↓
NAPOLI
1984-1991
APPS - 188, GLS - 81
↓
SEVILLA
1992-1993
APPS - 26, GLS - 5
↓
NEWELL'S OLD BOYS
1993-1994
APPS - 5, GLS - 0
↓
BOCA JUNIORS
1995-1997
APPS - 30, GLS - 7

Trophy Cabinet

WORLD CUP	X1
SERIE A CHAMPION	X2
ITALIAN CUP	X1
UEFA CUP	X1
SPANISH CUP	X1
ARGENTINIAN CHAMPION	X1

International Stats

CAPS	GOALS
91	34

BIOGRAPHY

BORN	OCT 30, 1960
NATIONALITY	ARGENTINIAN
STRONG FOOT	LEFT
HEIGHT	1.65M
RETIRED	1997

When Pelé was given the FIFA Player of the Century award, it was split between him and one other player—they just couldn't be separated. That man was Diego Maradona. Like Pelé, he took the world of football by storm in his prime, and the baby-blue and white stripes of Argentina became the shirt all the kids wanted in the 1980s.

Left-footed, small, strong, clever, skilful, a goalscorer, a leader and possibly the greatest dribbler in history—all of these traits and more can describe Maradona.

To Napoli and Argentina fans, he's an actual god. And to anyone who ever saw him play, he was simply on a different level.

Born on 30 October 1960 in Buenos Aires, Diego Armando Maradona and his large family lived in a shack in the middle of a shantytown*. They were poor and often hungry, but there was a lot of love and support. When Diego and his brothers showed early signs of football ability, it was encouraged.

He was first spotted by Argentinos Juniors, a club in Buenos Aires, and he was soon playing for their youth team. At 12, he was seen as a prodigy, and he would often come out onto the pitch at half-time during Argentinos games to entertain the crowd with his ball skills.

Between the start of 1973 and the end of '74, he led the youth team on a 141-game unbeaten run. Other future Argentina players were in that team, and it is widely considered the best collection of youth players in Argentina's history. During those early years, one of his biggest heroes was George Best.

Diego was so exceptional that Argentinos gave him his senior debut 10 days before he turned 16, making him the youngest player in the history of the Argentine Primera División. A few minutes into the game, he nutmegged an opposing defender, instantly bringing the crowd to their feet.

Two weeks after his 16th birthday, he scored his first senior goal.

Amazingly, he also made his international debut that year, playing for Argentina against Hungary at just 16. He would miss out on the 1978 World Cup after not making the squad, which is something he always hated. He was just 17 when the World Cup was played, but he knew he was good enough to be a part of it. His time would come!

In his five years with Argentinos Juniors, he scored 115 goals in 167 games, and in 1981, he moved to Boca Juniors, the biggest club in Argentina. He made his debut two days after signing, scoring twice in a 4–1 win, and he finished the year as a league champion. He was already a Boca Junior legend.

His time at Boca was short but sweet. As often happens, the big European clubs came calling. It was Barcelona who won out, paying a world-record fee for him.

That same summer, he led Argentina into the 1982 World Cup as they looked to defend their crown, having won it in '78. It didn't work out. Maradona was kicked from one end of the pitch to the other in every game, and they crashed out, having not won a game.

His time at Barcelona wasn't great, but he did win the Copa del Rey in 1983. That same year, he destroyed Real single-handedly at the Bernabéu, leaving the home fans in awe. They gave him a standing ovation, something that had never happened before and wouldn't happen again until Ronaldinho nearly two decades later.

Injuries and controversy followed him in his two years at Barca, and when the chance came to sign for lowly Napoli, he surprised everyone when he took it. Napoli were a mid-table team at best, and Maradona was in his prime, so the move didn't seem to make sense. It ended up being a match made in heaven. The Napoli crowd worshipped him, and he loved the attention.

He was soon given the armband, and after a while, he turned Napoli into title contenders. It's the same as one player being so good that they could join Crystal Palace and lead them to the league title. What he did at Napoli was genuinely scary.

At the 1986 World Cup, Maradona was at his peak. His couple of years in Naples, living among working-class people and playing for a team he loved, had helped him settle. He played every minute of the tournament, destroying every team he faced. It is easily the most dominant performance by one player at a World Cup.

He scored five and assisted five, including the greatest World Cup goal in history (some say the greatest goal, full stop), when he ran from inside his own half and beat most of the England team before rounding the keeper and scoring. In that same game, he scored another goal that will always be remembered when he punched the ball into the net. With no VAR back then, the goal stood!

In the final against West Germany, he was double-man-marked, something that has rarely, if ever, happened since. It didn't matter. He still wriggled free to set up the winning goal as Argentina won 3–2 to clinch the World Cup.

He returned to Napoli after the World Cup as the best and most famous player in the world. Still, nobody believed that he could actually make Napoli champions of Italy; it was just too outrageous. They didn't just win the league—Napoli won the double.

There were times during that season when it looked like Maradona was a man playing against boys. He genuinely won games on his own, sometimes drifting back into his own half to receive the ball, beating several players, and slamming the ball into the net. He scored free kicks, won penalties, assisted teammates and led the team with his passion and drive.

To show it wasn't a fluke, they won it again in 1990 after finishing runner-up the two previous seasons. Throughout all of this, Maradona battled drug addiction and the endless pressures of fame, but he always produced on the pitch. When he passed away in 2020, Napoli instantly retired his number 10 jersey and renamed their stadium the Stadio Diego Armando Maradona.

He had several massive bans (one was 15 months) after he left Napoli, and even though he played for a few other clubs before he retired, he was never the same. The Maradona who played for Napoli and Argentina throughout the 1980s was Messi, Cristiano Ronaldo and Ronaldo (R9) combined. He was simply phenomenal.

FINAL WHISTLE

Well, have you decided who is the best? Are you Messi or Ronaldo? Ronaldinho or Baggio? Maybe you're more old-school and think it's either Pelé or Maradona? See, it's not so easy, is it!

In truth, it would be pretty easy to fill a whole new book with 20 more of the greatest and still see nothing but legends because football has produced so many genius attacking players. That's how hard it is to decide!

There were surely players you felt should have been on the list, and maybe a few you believed didn't deserve their place, and that's cool. Football is for everyone, and that means that each fan gets to decide who they think is the best. Maybe you can make your own list for fun, then get your friends to do the same and compare! That would be a sure way to start some friendly arguments!

Most of the magic moments mentioned in this book can be found online, so be sure to look them up. Marco van Basten's volley against the Soviet Union in the final of Euro '88 deserves to be seen by every football fan. Maradona's solo run and finish against England at World Cup '86 is often called the greatest goal ever scored, and it just has to be seen to be believed.

For the more modern players such as Cristiano Ronaldo and Thierry Henry, there is an endless stream of highlight reels and "Best Tricks and Goals" videos on YouTube. Some of Di Stéfano's goals or Puskás's skills might be harder to find, but a lot of them are out there if you search for them.

You may have noticed that many of the players on the list came through hard times in their childhood before they reached the top. This just goes to show that all of us can achieve great things if we believe. We just have to keep our heads up and ask for help along the way!

Hopefully, you enjoyed learning about some of the greatest players in history. Between them, they have won everything in football, but more importantly, they all changed the game for the better. That's what legends do—they inspire the next generation to greatness!

GLOSSARY

ACL - The anterior cruciate ligament which connects the thigh to the shin. When it snaps, it's a very serious injury.

Ambassador - Someone who represents a country, business or association, such as a football club.

Baby Dream Team - The group of top players who came through Barcelona's La Masia academy in the period mentioned.

Bow-legged - A condition where a person's legs bend outward instead of straight down.

Clinical - Very efficient. When a striker is clinical, they rarely miss or feel pressure when in goal.

Defected - To leave your country and declare yourself a resident of another.

Endorsements - Getting paid to advertise, wear or promote a brand.

Favelas - Lower-class ghetto or slum houses. Usually shacks.

Feeder teams - Smaller clubs owned by bigger ones. They are usually used to loan out up-and-coming players so they can gain first team experience.

Flourished - Excelled, did well.

Futsal - A form of indoor or sometimes outdoor football that uses smaller teams and a smaller ball.

Galácticos - A term used for Real Madrid's team between 2000–06 when they tried to sign the best player in the world each summer.

Hormone deficiency - A condition when there aren't enough hormones in someone's blood. It can lead to growth problems.

Inaugural - The very first of something.

Journeyman - A player who plays for many different clubs during their career.

Malnourished - When someone isn't getting enough healthy food (or just not enough food).

Meniscus - An important part of the knee.

Parent club - The team that owns a feeder club.

Pichichi - Name of the top scorer award in Spain. It's the same as the Golden Boot or the Golden Shoe.

Prodigy - Someone who is exceptional at any given thing, such as maths, art or sport.

Prolific - Producing many of something. In football, it's someone who scores a lot of goals.

Pundits - Commentators or ex-players who talk about a sport.

Sextuple - Six trophies all won together.

Shantytown - An extremely poor area.

Soviet Union - Between 1922 and 1991, the Union of Soviet Socialist Republics (USSR) was the name of what is now known as Russia.

Squat - Short and wide.

Taça de Portugal - Portugal's main club cup competition. Similar to England's FA Cup.

Telegram - An earlier form of a fax, where a message was sent through a phone, and then written down and delivered to the person.

Trailblazer - Someone who sets the tone or creates a new way of doing something.

Understudy - A person who learns from someone else. In football, it would often be the younger player learning from the older one.

Verbal agreement - Not a true contract, but one agreed by two people through words.

West Germany - Germany was split into two following World War II and stayed as East and West Germany until the Berlin Wall came down in 1989. The countries didn't officially become one again until the following year.

Work permit - A form needed to be allowed to work in another country.

Work ethic - A determination to always work hard.

Worldies - A shortened version of "a world-class goal".

Printed in Great Britain
by Amazon